TANTROPATHY

MUDRAS, POSTURES AND MANTRAS FOR HEALTH, FITNESS AND HAPPINESS

TANTROPATHY

MUDRAS, POSTURES AND MANTRAS FOR HEALTH, FITNESS AND HAPPINESS

Dr. R. P. Upadhyay

An imprint of
B. Jain Publishers (P) Ltd.
USA — EUROPE — INDIA

First Indian Edition: 1999
5th Impression: 2012

Note from the Publishers
Any information given in this book is not intended to be taken as a replacement for medical advice. Any person with a condition requiring medical attention should consult a qualified practitioner or therapist.

All rights reserved. No part of this book may be reproduced, stored in a retrieval system or transmitted, in any form or by any means, mechanical, photocopying, recording or otherwise, without any prior written permission of the publisher.

© with the publisher

Published by Kuldeep Jain for
HEALTH  HARMONY
An imprint of
B. JAIN PUBLISHERS (P) LTD.
An ISO 9001 : 2000 Certified Company
1921/10, Chuna Mandi, Paharganj, New Delhi 110 055 (INDIA)
Tel.: +91-11-4567 1000 • *Fax*: +91-11-4567 1010
Email: info@bjain.com • *Website*: **www.bjain.com**

Printed in India by
J.J. Offset Printers

ISBN: 978-81-319-1837-1

PREFACE

Techniques of tantropathy are some of the possible breakthroughs in health care, fitness and happiness, that could definitely and dramatically alter our health in the near future. These are based on the age-old Indian cult, Tantra Yoga. There are three main schools of tantra: Hinduism tantra, Buddhism tantra and Jainism tantra. Tantropathy is based on all these schools. Nowadays ancient India's rich heritage is regaining its forgotten or lost significance in the light of modern researches and discoveries, and keeping pace with this changing tide is the technique of tantropathy in the field of health, hygiene and fitness. It is the technique of utilizing conscious energy or techniques of consciousness along with alternative medicines such as Mudras (Poses), Asanas (Postures), Yantras (Forms) and Mantras (Sacred Hymns). It is fully integrated in the new health care system. The system of tantropathy is discovered, invented and developed after going through the tantric systems of Hinduism, Jainism and Buddhism in particular, and the Tibetan and south-east Asian countries in general. The system represents a stress-free, conscious cleansing and detoxification method.

The techniques of tantropathy are designed to maintain cardiac, pulmonary, muscular, skeletal, fitness, psychological and spiritual fitness as well as nutritional fitness. Regular practice of these techniques can work wonders within a short span of time. Emotional and mental well being are as important as physical and, for that, uttering of some Mantra, listening to good music and keeping company with positive thinkers are quite conducive, as also assiduously avoiding negative thoughts and over-eating.

Ours is subjective approach with objective adjustment. This is the way of Indian synthetic thinking or spiritual approach towards the Self and the universe, whereas modern scientific thinking is an analytical or objective approach with subjective adjustment. Actually we all are seekers of pleasure, a state called in tantra "Anandam". We are internally guided by the pleasure principle, but tantra says: We must not avoid pleasure, We should accept and enjoy pleasure as God's blessing and select that on the basis of norms of age-old customs and cultures. The present book presents a systematic and model daily routine to attain this pleasure.

Man is born to work and prosper and affirm the virtue and wisdom of the humans striving for worldly happiness. "Brahm satyama gagadapisatyapekchetam", declares *Anand Sutram*. This world is relative truth, whereas Brahma is the absolute truth. Hence forbidding attitude to wordly virtues of pleasures is seen as unnatural and bleak for common people. But we should not forget that pleasure does not last long, because it is mixed with pain. Hence it should be regulated rationally and virtuously. Tantra says, "Nature has placed us under governance of two sovereign masters — pleasure and pain, and it is for us alone to determine what we shall do to maintain the balance between the two; it is a goal directed behaviour. In the words of Mr. Mill, a noted psychologist, "Not all pleasures are physical or bodily pleasures, but the human nature inherently enjoys the higher pleasures of the mind as well as the satisfaction of the intellectual, aesthetic and spiritual needs, which are not surely the glutton's provinces."

Tantra says, "The lasting happiness resides in the mind." Our mind is expressed through the three bodily channels — eyes, throat or vocal cord and muscles. Hence happiness may be enhanced or pain may be removed or reduced by the specific poses of these three sources. By this way you can become the master of your own pleasure and pain and even your fate (destiny). Our body is the microcosm of the universe. Hence practising the techniques of health, fitness, happiness and success enables the tapping of the energies from different bodily channels and nerve centres (chakras), and removing the general fatigue. These will certainly help you in becoming successful, attractive and healthy, and achieving a pleasing personality.

Getting up to work and doing the work satisfactorily are likely to give a feeling of well-being and happiness. Tantra believes in the power of inner and outer (muscular) strengths, both of which deserve equal weightage. A perfect body with perfect mental fitness and spiritual evolvement (social sense of duties and rights) represents the real health, fitness and happiness. I am a tantropath, and would advice to forego heavy routines and practice the techniques of tantropathy, which are basically auto-light-weight fitness exercises. For example, "Isht Pranam", a normal work-out programme, starts off with warming up the body only for 25 to 30 minutes.

Techniques of tantropathy, which I have discussed elaborately in this book, involve a series of complex therapeutic actions that flush out toxins from every cell of the body, which can be practiced by all persons — of all age groups and of either sex — who want a well toned body, appreciative mood and well disciplined life style. It is just a spiritual sport to play with oneself. This book is not written in a narrative style. It is more in the nature of an analysis into how the ideas of ancient India which the yogis, tantriks, rishis, munis and bhikshuks had propounded in the old days been changed and shaped significantly in the light of modern researches and discoveries, to what are now the techniques of tantropathy.

I have attempted to examine the human health problem in relation to three broad themes:

(1) to put forth the structure and curative possibilities of different postures, poses and forms (asanas, mudras and yantras), in unison and sequence,

(2) to unfold a new technique of tantropathy on the basis of traditional tantric prevention-and-cure in the light of modern researches and discoveries,

(3) and to exhibit a naturo-psycho-physico-spirituo system for getting healthy, successful, magnetic and with pleasing personality.

It will not be out of place to mention here that the body has enormous recuperative powers, and the techniques of tantropathy give the body enough scope to heal itself. Hence the first week for the techniques will be the preparatory stage, the second week the conciliatory stage, the third week the recuperative stage, and the fourth week and onward will be the health, fitness and happiness stage.

We used Shubh Bhawana technique on the basis of Atharvaveda (4.13.6.7) or the technique of self-hypnosis and auto suggestion, which are discussed elaborately in this book. We have also devoted one chapter of this book on observational meditation, which is an experimental procedure for spiritual evolution and therapeutic qualities of human body and mind. As Muni Kishan Lal says in his book, *Postures of Hands: Application and Impact,* "Postures influence life and behaviour of a person; postures are reflections of sentiments and sentiments are reflections of postures."

It is encouraging that revival of old values seems to be gaining momentum nowadays in the Western as well as Indian society. There are several instances where modern medicines could provide only symptomatic relief and the benefits derived are temporary in nature. My past experience has shown that at places where conventional therapies could not work, alternative medicines have been helpful. You will also get rid of the tedious process of all kinds of tests and long prescription of expensive medicines. No doubt, by avoiding allopathic system of medicines, the biggest comfort of a human being is a trouble-free life.

Though modern medicines are capable of curing many complicated ailments, their inherent side-effects and high cost of treatment are fastly making them out of reach of the common people. This accounts for the popularity of alternative therapies like tantropathy, because not only are they cost effective, but also they have virtually no side-effect.

The practice of the techniques of tantropathy, if learnt and done properly as well as regularly, can be used effectively for self-healing as well as for community service. This system has proved effective beyond doubt even for chronic ailments like migraine, sciatica, diabetes, asthma and obesity in general and relaxation in particular.

::::::::

CONTENTS

CHAPTER 1 ....(1-80)

- Mind and body healing 2
- Poses and postures of hand: their application and impact .. 8
- Postures and poses: natural expression 10
- Beginning of postures and poses 11
- Expression of feelings through dance poses 12
- Simple man of ancient times 15
- Importance of postures and poses 16
- Hath yoga and poses 18
- Mudras: switch-board of body 21
- Effect of poses on body 23
- Mudras are windows to spirituality 24
- Body: a conglomeration of atoms 26
- Homogeneous atomic assembly and mudras 29
- Poses and divine power 31
- Elements of yoga and poses 32
- Surya mudra (sun posture) 35
- Gyan mudra (posture of knowledge) 38
- Vayu mudra (air posture) 42
- Akash mudra (sky posture) 45
- Prithvi mudra (earth posture) 48
- Varun mudra (water posture) 51
- Apaan mudra (flatus posture) 53
- Pran mudra (vital air posture) 56
- Angushtha mudra (thumb posture) 59
- Surabhi mudra (fragrance posture) 61
- Mrigi mudra (antelope posture) 66
- Hansi mudra (laughter posture) 68
- Shankh mudra (shell posture) 70
- Pankaj mudra (lotus posture) 73

- Anushasan mudra (discipline posture) 75
- Samanvay mudra (co-ordination posture) 77
- Veetrag mudra (dispassionate posture) 79

CHAPTER 2 ....(81-114)
- How do techniques of tantropathy work? 82

CHAPTER 3 ....(115-178)
- Sleeplessness vs sound sleeping 116
- Stress reaction vs relaxation response 128
- General fatigue vs life style 143
- Cure constipation, heart burn and headache through toning up of abdominal and rectal muscles 152
- Headache 161
- Control of diabetes and impotency through tantropathy 166
- Chandrayan technique for obesity 171

CHAPTER 4 ....(179-241)
- Techniques of tantropathy 180
- Nirmimekh varjan technique 185
- 'Isht Pranam' technique..191
- Angari technique (hanging loosely) 208
- Prasanna kriti and hasya kriti 212
- Gyan-dhyan mudra technique 216
- Auto-suggestion technique in self hypnosis 218
- Meditation technique..222
- Model life style for health and fitness 225
- Good health is our nature 235

PRESENTATION

To,

Shri Shyamsundar Rasiwashiya

*"You have always been so very kind,
You have helped in every way,
Turned tears to happy laughter,
Brightened up a lovely day."*

With Love and Affection
R. P. Upadhyay

CHAPTER 1

- Mind and body healing 2
- Poses and postures of hand: their application and impact 8
- Postures and poses: natural expression 10
- Beginning of postures and poses 11
- Expression of feelings through dance poses 12
- Simple man of ancient times 15
- Importance of postures and poses 16
- Hath yoga and poses 18
- Mudras: switch-board of body 21
- Effect of poses on body.................................23
- Mudras are windows to spirituality..................24
- Body: a conglomeration of atoms 26
- Homogeneous atomic assembly and mudras ...29
- Poses and divine power 31
- Elements of yoga and poses 32
- Surya mudra (sun posture) 35
- Gyan mudra (posture of knowledge) 38
- Vayu mudra (air posture)................................42
- Akash mudra (sky posture) 45
- Prithvi mudra (earth posture) 48
- Varun mudra (water posture) 51
- Apaan mudra (flatus posture) 53
- Prana mudra (vital air posture) 56
- Angushtha mudra (thumb posture) 59
- Surabhi mudra (fragrance posture) 61
- Mrigi mudra (antelope posture) 66
- Hansi mudra (laughter posture).......................68
- Shankh mudra (shell posture) 70
- Pankaj mudra (lotus posture) 73
- Anushasan mudra (discipline posture) 75
- Samanvay mudra (co-ordination posture).........77
- Veetrag mudra (dispassionate posture)............79

MIND AND BODY HEALING

Mind and body are dependent entirely on each other: linked and closely associated, they supplement, complement and co-ordinate mutually. In Tantra texts we find a statement, 'Bubhukshati kim na karoti papam', much in the same way as the well known French saying 'Cuisine et Culture', meaning that thought depends on the stomach. How can a hungry man be prevented from committing a crime? However, those with the best of stomachs are not always the best thinkers. The revered philosophical masters of Japan, Okada Torojero and Koneku Sosiki have accepted the superiority of the belly region over the much venerated place of the brain, chest, heart and the spine. "Spine is the shrine of divine", they say, pointing to the belly region. Some few centimetres below the human navel, belly is the human centre of gravity. The intellect, the will and the emotion within the brain, the chest and heart should not debar the anchorage of life in the belly to play its rightful role."

As we know, the brain is the seat of thought, memory, emotions and, above all, intelligence. Nature has taken billions of years to progress from brainless microscopic life forms to the complex brain of human beings. The bacteria and other micro-organisms are intelligent enough to learn and able to survive even after administration of antibiotics, capable to mutate to the forms that go undetected by man's immune system. It is unlikely that they are able to ever think of a plan to get more out of their life. Actually they are driven purely by the instinct of survival.

At the other extreme of life's spectrum, man possesses intelligence that goes beyond the survival instinct and has the capacity to explore avenues that are totally alien to the rest of the animal kingdom. And today we see the prized possession of human body and brain, which has developed science, art, music and what not. We can describe brain as a physical entity on the basis of size, shape and structure. But intelligence still remains a metaphysical concept within the purview of both scientists and philosophers. Laying stress on the mind-body connections, doctors say that the mind is directly linked to the physical body. Internal anxiety, fear and grief are associated with high blood pressure. Anger, jealousy and hatred are major risk factors for heart attack and paralysis. These problems can be tackled by practising the techniques of tantropathy.

So, what is it about our brains that makes us intelligent enough not only to survive but also to become physically fit, mentally balanced, emotionally stable and spiritually evolved? Memory gives us the capacity to recollect information and to forget unnecessary things, including past experiences. This is the mystery of human intelligence, which is termed phenomenal memory, the building blocks of the brain. The more the neurons, the more their interconnections called synapses, the faster the brain becomes in its ability to process information. Any further improvement in the brain would require larger neurons with more effective synapses. A thicker insulation, called myelin, would be required to insulate the neurons effectively from accidental cross-talk. Practice of "Chakra-Shodhan-Bhedan" technique of tantropathy, which is a combination of 'Deva Mudra' and 'Pashu Mudra' along with 'Dharna-Dhyan' technique, helps produce myelin in sufficient quantity to insulate and enlarge the neurons. Dharna-Dhyan technique of tantropathy is the "Karam-Gyan Udbodhan Vidhi" or Hobby formation technique.

Our behaviour is controlled by our chemical transmitter system secreted on neurons in our brain. The brain spreads out its fibres to arouse reaction and myelin. A thicker insulation is produced after concentration under pleasant light whether morning sunlight, the moon light or candle light while performing "Deva mudra" (Divine pose) even for 5 minutes. Tantra declares "Pitri yagya" must be performed after taking full bath in light and without wiping the body with towel, in the morning with the offering poses (Arpanatmak mudra) for health, fitness and happiness. Thus it reveals the scientific basis of our age-old techniques of tantra.

Further Tantra says, "It is action which influences our intelligence, memory and emotions and controls physical and mental problems. It is only action which makes a man perfect physically, mentally and spiritually. Be great by your selfless service, sincere practice of the techniques of tantropathy and sacrifice something from your earnings for the society."

"If you want to be great, meditate on Great (Supreme consciousness), and your all the faculty of brain develops miraculously", says Shri P. R. Sarkar, a great tantrik of 20th century. By practising these techniques regularly, changing the style of life by adopting the daily routine mentioned in the book and following the dietary habits based on "amritann" fruits and green vegetables, one can certainly prevent diseases and cure even prolonged ailments.

TANTROPATHY

Actually your physical, mental and spiritual health depends on brain and body chemicals. Regular practice of the techniques of tantropathy alters the brain chemistry. It slows down the action of the systematic nervous system in practical terms. Your body does not get flooded with stress hormones as quickly as before. Your blood pressure does not rise every time. If you have an argument, your heart does not start pounding for fear of missing the bus. It also improves the functioning of the Parasympathetic system, which controls your ability to relax. Even after a period of stress, you will be able to relax and normalise quickly. Blood pressure comes down, the heart rate returns to normal and breathing becomes slow and deep.

Tense muscles send uneasy stress signals to the brain, but once they are gently stretched in proper postures and poses of the techniques of tantropathy, the signals are automatically switched off. Over time the tantric poses also stimulate sluggish glands into operating more efficiently, and chemical balance of mind and body is restored. That may explain why techniques of tantropathy can bring down stress-related diabetes, high blood pressure and heart diseases. It works through mind-body connections This mind-body tie of relation is knotted lightly but lovingly. That is why tantropathy becomes stress-free cleansing and detoxification technique through a novel combination of yogic postures and tantric poses.

Today due to pollution and additives in the food we consume, our bodies get bogged down with substances that cause health problems. Due to mind-body relation knotted tightly through the tantrik techniques, a series of complex therapeutic actions flush out toxins from every cell of the body; and once the morbidity caused by the toxins is eliminated, one becomes healthy or the diseases vanish. It is however necessary to follow regular daily schedule.

Recent researches show that our body has more than 100 biological rhythms that cycle every 24 hours, called circadian rhythms, which modify the body functions, such as the heart rate, hormone levels, temperature, pain threshold and blood pressure. Our brain regulates most of the cells that set these rhythms according to outside influences, such as daylight and darkness. Outside influences are meal-time, visit to toilet, doing exercises, sleep and even contact with other people. When you cannot keep your normal routine, make your every effort to return to it or establish a new one. Tantra says, "Keep your daily routine constant and be healthy and happy." It is now scientifically proved that keeping the daily routine constant is the basis of healthy style of life. If you want to avoid jetlag (khumari), you have to perform other daily duties and activities as regular as visiting toilet, eating and sleeping etc.; the activities from visiting toilet to going to bed are called puja in Tantra.

Puja (worshipping) involves body, mind and spirit. Tantra says our body is a yantra and that is enveloped by ethereal body (Sukhshma sharir) and the mental body (Atisukhshma sharir). Our physical body is a symptomatic body, whereas mental body is emotional symbolic body, and spiritual body is imaginative (Bimbatmak) body. We become ill first in spiritual body, and then negative, passimistic and inactive images become dominant over positive, optimistic and creative images. These distorted images of spiritual body compel the mental body to become emotional and produce similar thoughts. After that, symptoms of diseases are seen on physical body and we become ill. 'Mudra, mantra mayang yantram', that is mudras and mantras influence all the three yantras (spiritual, mental and physical). Hence illness can be treated on all three levels by practising proper postures. The practice of mudra and mantra daily can develop integrated personality by this way involving physical, mental and spiritual bodies.

POSES AND POSTURES OF HAND: THEIR APPLICATION AND IMPACT

Body has its own language, and the postures and poses appearing on it express innermost feelings of the man. The body expresses these feelings in its own way. Postures are the sitting, standing and laying positions of the body, whereas poses are the expression of our mind through its three main body channels — eyes and facial poses; vocal cord, its tune of expression (Bakhari, Madyama and Pashyanti), and muscles especially of hands and finger. If a man is very angry, his anger will peep through his eyes first, after a few seconds vocal cord will be affected and then after a few seconds there would be visible expression of muscles of hand and fingers in fighting pose. Yoga gives emphasis on postures and Dhyana, whereas Tantra relies more on poses and Dharna. Dhyana is the wastage of time and energy. And postures without Deva mudra and Pashu Mudra (poses) are lifeless positions without any bodily expression.

Although with the increasing use of language the indicative body language has gone into oblivion, the body has not lost sight of its duty. Mind and body may fail to register an incident, but the body mechanism expresses it without fail. Face is the index of emotions. However lightly or humorously anything is said, whether the mind likes it or not, the face expresses the emotions. Though the mind may try hard to conceal emotions, the expressions on the face reveal these and the body feels uneasiness.

A boy, Mukesh is deeply perturbed why his body is feeling uneasy without any reason. He had to do something for that but failed miserably. He is trying again and again to remember what he had missed? Perhaps he had forgotten to close the water tap? Did he bring any valuables from the shop and has he left them somewhere? His body is a witness to that particular incident. It wanted to inform the mind immediately, but there was lack of coordination between the mind and the body language, which led the boy in a state of tension. His tension would not end till the unfinished job is properly settled. The boy was doing effort more and more to relax from the tension, but in return he suffered more than before. It is just similar to the efforts of a boy who while trying to untie his trouser-string, pulls the wrong end of the string, resulting in the knot getting more complicated. He has to reverse the process of tying the knot, then alone he will be able to untie the knot.

The tension reflecting on the body can be eliminated only through the process of reversal to get to the root of the tension. One has to follow the process of returning to the past, which is known as reversal or Pratikraman yoga. As you travel back in your memories and as this journey reaches the point of incidence, body shivers and the incidence clearly appears in the memory. The body immediately gets rid of the tension. As soon as in his journey into the memory lane Mukesh reaches the garage, he immediately realises that he has left the keys of the vehicle inside it, the tension begins to melt and vanish within no time. He telephoned his family and explained the situation. When he was informed from his residence about taking out the key from the vehicle and the garage being locked, the tension evaporated totally.

POSTURES AND POSES: NATURAL EXPRESSION

Some postures and poses are natural; whenever circumstances develop a person knowingly or unknowingly adopts proper postures and poses in a particular situation or circumstance. If a man is worried, he immediately but unintentionally expresses his worries through his postures. He would sit loosely and his hands will touch his forehead or he will rest his chin on his hands. After seeing such a man, anyone can easily understand that the man is deeply worried. If you fail to recollect the answer to a question you will automatically start staring towards the sky or roof. By this posture of staring, you are trying to sharpen your memory. Similarly, heating palms etc. are natural poses that effortlessly appear on human body in certain situations or circumstances. These are natural phenomena. Now the universities impart training of these natural postures and poses and a man uses these poses effortlessly and unconsciously.

When you feel cold, your hands automatically unite and you put them under your armpits. Similar postures and poses are used to exhibit vanity and pride. Similarly, to express humbleness a man folds his hands and stays in this pose either in standing or sitting postures. Whenever a man keeps his fists under his armpits, a sense of vanity creeps in, and when these hands are folded in to Abhinandanatmak mudra (welcome pose), he reflects the feeling of humbleness.

BEGINNING OF POSTURES AND POSES

The development of postures and poses in Indian civilisation dates back to primitive age. In those days language was not so much developed and the ancient men were using signs, illustrations and diagrams (Pratik) for communicating their feelings among themselves and with each other. Rishabh Dev was known as Adinath or Baba Adam. He had two daughters — Brahmi and Sundari. The script that Adinath taught his daughter Brahmi, later came to be known as Brahmi script. The second daughter Sundari was trained in other few arts including dance. The postures and poses in dance are so expressed that the entire emotions get mentally assimilated. The reality, which can be expressed through postures in a moment, needs a long statement when words are used to communicate it. Various subtle expressions of mudra (poses) express the entire range of emotions through the body. Here not only the body adapts itself to the different postures and poses but the whole of the consciousness gets transformed into that very form. Thus the consciousness expresses its feelings through various dance postures.

::::::::

EXPRESSION OF FEELINGS THROUGH DANCE POSES

The Indian dances actually developed not for the sole objective of entertainment but for the expression of emotions aesthetically. The movements of body give rise to postures and expressions of eyes, facial and hand muscles. This subtle feeling is Mudra. We cannot separate postures from poses for general purposes, especially in dance. A dancer uses his or her hands to form various postures and poses and is overpowered by the corresponding feelings and emotions. The postures and poses in a dance indicate the expressions of the dancer.

The movement of feet is called 'Pad Vikshepa'. Various applications of ankle-bells (ghungharu) along with feet movement are also made in order to give synthetic dimensions to the sound of anklebells; the joints of legs, heels, knees and thighs are kept in motion; and the leg-joints are kept in different postures. This is known as 'chari', which is of 30 types. These are divided into two broad types: Bhumichari and Aakashchari. In Bhumichari the feet touch the ground and through it different postures are exhibited. In Aakashchari one foot is placed on the ground and the other is kept suspended in the air.

In dance, 24 different emotions are expressed through various hand postures. The emotions expressed through these postures have been defined in the book *Sangit Ratnakar*. These postures and poses may be called the indicative language in the world of dance. The names and the emotions expressed by each of the postures are given below.

- Pataka: flag, sum, king's palace, cold sound
- Tripataka: sunset, address, body, begging
- Hanspaksha: friend, mountain, moon, air, hair, calling
- Mudrakhya: ocean, heaven, death, meditation, memory, whole
- Ardhachandra: why, where, sky, God, beginning
- Makar: ray, fly, bangle, veda
- Suchimukh: eyebrow, tail, hoping, world, mouth
- Hansasya: vision, bright, red, black line
- Shikhar: path, eye, leg, walking, searching
- Arnalabha: tiger, horse, lotus, ice, fruit
- Mukul: monkey, wolf, fragile
- Shuktund: bird
- Kartarimuka: male, house, sin, brahmin, purity
- Mrigshursh: dear
- Anjali: fire, horse, lion, rage, rain, branch
- Bardhman: ear-ring, well, the great vow, ascetic
- Pallava: buffalo, evidence, condition, smoke, thunder bolt (vajra)
- Kapithak: touching, net, massage, wandering, page
- Sarpashir: snake
- Katak mukh: bending, killing with an arrow
- Kakatak: Krishna, Vishnu, gold, mirror, woman
- Bramara: ears of elephant, umbrella
- Masti: order, minister, medicine, blessing, soul
- Araal: tree, diot, wicked

"Hasta Pataka Mudrakhya,
Katako Mustiriltyapi |
Kartarimukh Shankhashcha,
Shykatund Kapithakah ||

Hans pakshshcha Shikharopi,
Hansaya Punrogati |
Ardhchandrashacha Mukuto,
Bhramaarah Shuychika Mukhah ||

Pallava Rikta Patakashach,
Mrigshirsah Haidayastatha |
Punah Sarpshir Saugyo,
Vardhamanaka Ityapi ||

Aral Arnanamasheh,
Mukula Katka Mukh ||
Chaturvishanti Rilyaiva,
Karslastra Sabhyata ||

— *Sangit Ratnakar*

SIMPLE MAN OF ANCIENT TIMES

Primitive people had direct contact with the nature. His behaviour, whether from within or outwardly, was always uniform. Whatever he did he used to do it in totality. He never did any thing incompletely. His rage too was never incomplete. Why to hide one's rage behind the facade of apology. It was the collected knowledge of the mind, that made the man wily. This led the man to start a life of deceits and lies. He enters into a new era of acting. This duality of life is the root cause of sufferings and seed of miseries. The only path of salvation from all this is that he should become natural, simple and uniform. Simplicity and neutrality are never learnt, nor can these be acted as a role. If anybody tries to act, the consequences are always horrible and amount to fraud. In such circumstances the outer postures and poses of a man are different, whereas his inner indications express something different, which leads to conflicting situations.

The general tendencies of primitive man were the same as of the modern people, but he used to possess the bitter traits like anger, prestige, attachment and hatred in lesser quantity.

As such his behaviour and conduct used to be straight. The mildness in bitterness makes a man simple and humble. He behaves as a normal person. This was the beauty of the native man's simplicity. The people neither wore clothes nor adorned themselves with ornaments, yet their divinity was second to none. They used to express their emotions through their postures and poses.

IMPORTANCE OF POSTURES AND POSES

Various types of 'Asanas' are positions of the body and the poses are the communications of higher and finer stage of emotions and feelings which are expressed through bodily postures. Hence the emergence of microvibrations within the body are poses, which can be compared to the micro-sound of a word, the "Naad". During meditation in a particular posture (asana), when the emergence of poses becomes natural and easy, the meditator starts progressing towards this path. This is not his madness, but the reaction of energy produced within him and the expression of his emotions under such conditions. The meditation should be performed under the guidance of an able teacher. This energy can be controlled and emotions can be pacified by meditation. This can be transformed into determination, retreat and concentration. This energy is led into Sushumna, one of the principle nerves of human body, and can be made to move vertically upward. Thus the dormant vitality (Pran Shakti) can be awakened. The *Hath Yoga Pradipika* says that without arousing the vitality the chakras (circles) cannot be pierced. The practice of postures and poses is one of the ways of awakening the dormant vitality in the energy centre. These affect subtle body (Sukhshma Sharir) which activates the Prana body. Without posture, poses cannot be performed, and without poses, postures are only dead positions. Postures and poses are meant not only for physical and mental attainment, but are used also for higher spiritual evolution. The importance of postures and poses is explained in *Gherand Samhita*, as:

"Idam tu Mudra Patalama,
Kathitam Chandkaple I
Ballabham Sarvasidhanam,
Jara Marnanasakam" I I

It means: O Chand Kapala! These poses are liked and loved by all siddhas. It is the conqueror of death and destroyer of old age.

Poses are unlimited in number like asanas, and some of these postures are discussed in this book for health, fitness and happiness or for attaining successful, attractive, healthy and pleasing personality even in this modern competitive and complicated age.

HATH YOGA AND POSES

The 'Hath' yoga is made up of two words 'Ha + tha'. There are two important nerves, Ida and Pingla, running parallel to Sushumna in our spine. Ida represents "Ha" and Pingla "Tha" as well as moon and sun. According to Hathyoga scriptures, fusion of the moon and the sun strengthens the path of Sushumna and opens the path of the practitioner for higher experiences. Basically, in tantric traditions the Kundalini, which lies dormant in "Muladhar Chakra" like a coiled serpent, becomes active after unification of "Hatha" (Ida and Pingla) and travels from Muladhar Chakra to Agya Chakra, crossing Swadhsthan, Manipur and Anahad Chakra up to 'Nad', 'Bindu' and 'Kala' and introduces the yogi to the energy and knowledge of self.

Several treatises on Hathyoga, such as *Hathyoga Pradipika, Grakh Paddhati* and *Shir Samhita* describe methods of making the body strong and mind stable for attaining perfection in meditation. These include stages from purification to the highest state of the body and mind. Man possesses a developed mind with hidden unlimited potential, and with the practice of postures and poses one can unveil these faculties after achieving perfection in meditation. Meditation has been discussed impressively in *Gherand Samhita*. Basically all the forms of meditation are not very difficult, but under the guidance of an experienced teacher, one can achieve the higher stage of meditation. A comprehensive and unique analysis of different postures and poses by yogis is also given in the book dealing with consciousness.

Two types of poses

There are two types of poses — gross and subtle — which can be called Pashu Mudra and Deva Mudra or Hathayoga Mudra and Yoga Mudra.

Hathayoga poses are defined differently in different books. Names of 25 different poses as per *Gherand Samhita, Hathyoga Pradipika* and *Shiva Samhita* are:

"Maha Mudra Nabho Mudra
Udiyan Galandharam I

Vipritkarini Yoni,
Bajili Shakti Chalino I

Tadagi Mandvi Mudra,
Shambhavi Ponch Dharna I

Ashvini Pashini Kaka,
Matangi Cha Bhujangini I

Panchvishti Mudraiva,
Sidhidasheheh Yoginam" I

Maha mudra, Nabho mudra, Udiyam, Jalaadhar, Mulbandh, Mahavedh, Khechari, Viparit Karni, Yoni, Vajroli, Shakti, Taragi, Mandvi, Shambhavi, Panchdharn, Ashwini, Pashini Kaka, Mataangi and Bhujangini.

One can achieve attainment (siddhi) by practising these poses mentioned above. These are known to be helpful in awakening the six chakras. But there are processes of Hatha Yoga which are entirely different from the subtle elemental processes. It is a bit difficult process, for which an experienced yogi's assistance will be required.

These poses are the combination of Asana, Poses, Pranayams, Knots and Contemplations. Hence it is not useful for common people to practice these poses, and for this proper training and close supervision are required.

MUDRAS: SWITCH-BOARD OF BODY

The world of senses is gross. Senses are utilised every moment. We are aware of its impressions and sensitivities. The world of emotions, on the contrary, is subtle and for its comprehension subtle observation is required, and hence intellect is found rarely. When our feelings are expressed through our poses, we recognise them. Poses are the impressions of feelings on our body, which are explained by experienced yogis and tantrics. Mental feeling produces corresponding bodily poses (mudras) and the mudras produce corresponding feelings in the mind. It is a double-way traffic. Our body is made up of five elements and if these elements become unbalanced we suffer from different physical and mental ailments. Practice of poses balances it. Poses are the switch-board of our body and mind. They act as catalyst in awakening the consciousness. Mudras (poses) are effective instantly, but sometimes their impact on body and mind manifests gradually after regular practice. As acupressure helps in making different organs of the body healthy, the poses are auto pressures for balancing the five elements of our body and for making it orderly and balanced. They are immediately helpful in changing the mood, temperament and even personality traits. Lord Mahavir and Lord Buddha used Abhaya Mudra before the masses and attracted them through their personal magnetism, leading them toward fearlessness and non-violence beyond expectation while exemplifying fearlessness, equality and non-violence.

The conditions of body and mind are also observed closely through mudras apart from highlighting in accordance with mudra. Mudra is one of the means of meditation. Without proper mudra, meditation is not possible.

::::::

EFFECT OF POSES ON BODY

Spiritual evolution has led to germination of the seed of heavenly knowledge in man. This knowledge has helped him in understanding equally the inner and outer worlds. Human body consists of thousands of nerves, arteries and veins, apart from several organs etc. which are connected or related internally. This was known to Indian Rishis and Munis. They knew and experienced that consciousness of human being has unlimited energy, knowledge and Anandam. It can be developed by purifying the nerves through exhibition of mudras. Postures, poses, breathing exercises, meditation and penance were invented and researched upon by them for the benefit of common people as well as the aspirants of higher pursuits. Removal of excreta and disorders purify that nerves and veins on one hand and leads to knowledge, energy and joy of consciousness on the other.

::::::::

MUDRAS ARE WINDOWS TO SPIRITUALITY

Our senses are always used in a planned manner, and are vested with energy and capacity. They always hanker for attraction, beauty, sound, smell, taste and touch, and derive the maximum pleasure by doing these activities. But these senses of enjoyment are temporary, transient and short lived, and gradually detachment and transformation takes place automatically. These are extrovert traits of our personality which mislead the mind and body both. However, the extroversion of our senses expresses mudras of subtle feeling of consciousness on body and mind, and influences not only the person himself but the people around him, as revealed through Abhaya Mudra of Lord Mahavira and Lord Buddha.

American scientists have researched and studied the language of body and its mechanism. Eugin-Djendalin is the prominent among those scientists. Although a common man is unable to understand the language of the body, he is aware of the sense conveyed through it. It is beyond his realm to understand and analyse the body language. He calls it "felt sense" and he is engaged in its scientific analysis. A number of psychologists like E.D. Elperson and J.P. Gray are also engaged seriously to know more about it. They are of the opinion that the moment we understand the language of felt sense, our relations undergo unimaginable transformation. They believe that our body has a special graph of our personality, which alone acts as a bridge between the relations of two persons. Relations are established with the man who agrees with the graph. Relations cannot be formed with a man of different graph and such a person is considered misunderstood, but it is not necessary that such a man is really wrong. One considers such a person wrong (though he may be absolutely right) simply because his graph does not tally with that of others. This is the reason why such persons do not develop cordial relations. When we meet a person and confront him, our body starts acting in a dramatic way. We feel a kind of sensation, sensitiveness and shivering in our body. Some parts of limbs and organs start throbbing and quivering. The body becomes miserable and stooped, sometimes it becomes stiff. All these are the languages of the body. Now the scientists are analysing this language. Complexes of inferiority and superiority in a man weaken his personality. Two children of a mother have been seen with different birth traits in spite of oneness. The "felt-sense graph", which is inborn in a child plays a major role in the development of his personality. Psychologists have devised a method to code this felt sense, which they call "focusing" method. Under this method through focusing of consciousness on memory, the light of consciousness is spread over emotional experience. Thus emotional experiences of the past and learned feeling of consciousness are clearly separated from each other. This can determine a gap between the viewer and the view. This method is comparable to the manifestation of past memories during contemplation, which is similar to "Jati Smriti" of tantra.

::::::::

BODY: A CONGLOMERATION OF ATOMS

The moment a creature is born in a form, it has to accept new atoms for its safety and evolution. This acceptance of atoms is technically called "food sufficiency". Food consists of atom bodies, in whose absence the living being can neither build its body nor can develop it. Senses are also developed along with bodies. First the creatures develop the sense of touch. Thereafter, in accordance with its chromosomes, it starts developing its senses of taste, smell, sight and hearing. On the basis of these senses, the living beings are known as the beings with single senses, double senses or five senses. The bodies of these living beings get transformed into lifeless bodies after death.

Earth, water, fire, air and sky are called five basic elements (panch bhuta) as per vedic philosophy. This philosophy considers that these five basic elements are the basis of creation of the entire universe, and it is in the dissolution of these elements that the universe ends. Excess and deficiency of these five elements in the body leads to various diseases and disorders. Our health is the balance of state of these elements. This single truth has been interpreted from two different angles. In Jain philosophy the union of the living being and the conglomeration of atoms is considered to be the basis of creation and disintegration of atoms is known as destruction, whereas the vedic philosophy says that union of gross five elements is the birth and disintegration is the basis of destruction.

Radiated atomic mass

Atoms are continuously radiated from both the conscious and unconscious bodies (living and non-living bodies). Both the bodies have their own shape of installations (Sansthan). The energy emitting out of these bodies is radiated as per the shapes of installations and has its own effect. The shapes of installations (Sansthan) are mainly circular, global, triangular, quadrangular, bulk (Ayatam) etc.

- Circle (Brit) : Circular (like a ball)
- Round (Parimandal) : Round (like a bangle)
- Triangular (Trinsh) : Triangular
- Rectangular (Chaturans) : Rectangular
- Bulk (Aayaan) : Shape of prolonged rules.

According to the shape and size of the installation (Sansthan), the aura emits its fascimile or its energy radiates. Since identical shapes are emitted out of it, it has a broad effect. The application of yantra prepared by Sadhana with will power through mantras, make it spirited and energised. Similarly, poses (mudras) specified by spirited person with awakened spirits creates sansthan of its own by exhibiting mudras. As hands and other parts of the body create mudras, they also provide opportunity and give a chance to atoms of different elements scattered in the universe to adopt the shape and be influenced by it for getting healthy, successful, attractive and with a pleasing personality. These poses are not merely shapes but these are spirited postures which emit various elemental forces affecting man. It is necessary to use and apply reason while practising the use of poses (mudra) because it may lead to evolution as well as destruction of energy and other characteristics of human beings.

As per Jain philosophy, there are five senses: Shrotra (ear), Chakshu (eyes), Ghran (nose), Rasa (taste) and Sparsh (touch). These are the means of establishing relation and contact with the mind, body and voice internally as well as externally. There are three objectives behind this relation and contact (of senses with mind, body and voice), which are: to act or doing by oneself, to make others act or dictating others to do that, and to approve for testifying and justifying the fact. When a man tries to do some thing with these three contacts (yoga), poses are created automatically and expressed accordingly through his face and body (eye, voice and muscles). These poses are created after observing and assimilating atoms of 5 elements, which are the conglomeration of different types.

::::::::

HOMOGENEOUS ATOMIC ASSEMBLY AND MUDRAS

Homogeneous atomic assembly is known as 'Vergana', a technical word of Jainism, which is divided into 8 categories: 5 of the body and one each for speech, mind and breath, as given below:

- The body is made up of flesh, bones and marrows — Audarik Vergana.
- The body is made up of specific figulesers by contemplation — Aaharik Vergana.
- The body is made up of specific atom mass by the God of hell — Vaikriya Vergana.
- The body is made up of energy — Tejas Vergana.
- The body is made up of active atoms — Karmana Vergana.
- Atoms capable of assumption by lauguage of feeling and emotion (Bhasha) — Bhasha Vergana.
- Contemplable and understanding atoms of another person's mind — Mana Vergana.
- Atom wings which one uses in breathing process — Shwasochchhas Vergana.

These verganas are of two types — gross and subtle. Cold, hot, smooth and coarse touch are the subtle verganas. There are eight touch senses of gross verganas — cold, hot, smooth, coarse, small, loose, gentle and harsh. When the atom wings of subtle verganas are expressed and transmitted outwardly, they become gross verganas. There is close relation between poses and verganas. The form of conglomeraion of verganas takes the same shape of poses (mudras) that we have at the time of acceptance of the verganas and as such there is an established correlation between verganas and poses.

Poses affect the nerves and mechanism of glands of a person in the same way as the atmosphere affects a person. After assuming the shapes of identical atoms, poses radiate and continue to appear from the body and influence the inner self of the person as well as the atmosphere, leading to this transformation.

::::::::

POSES AND DIVINE POWER

All the gods and goddesses possess and are equipped with divine powers as well as have their own specific poses (Mudras). If such poses are created, posed and expressed by any individual, that will work as signal for transmitting divine powers to the person for health, fitness and happiness. Similarly, Vedas and tantra have also declared that Mudras with invocation of Mantra sound also attract and transmit divine powers and influence the individual as well as atmosphere.

What is Mantra? A man is identified by his name and style of life or the code or words and the behaviour. Secret informations are passed on by using code words by army usually. Army is deployed or retreats using these code words. Similarly, for invocation of God and for radiating godly powers and energies, indication sounds of causative words of five fundamental matters of universe are used as Mantra. Lang (earth), wang (water), Rang (fire), Yang (sky) and Hang (air), are called Mantra, representing different matters and their energies. Aum is the common and combined word for these words and is treated as Mantra. These are also indicative words of Mudras. Poses not only bring changes in body and mind, but also create a gentle and hypnotic atmosphere, which facilitates transmission of the divine powers and energies.

ELEMENTS OF YOGA AND POSES

The human body is not only just a being of flesh and bones but is a powerful medium of outflow of knowledge and energy. The element of self, imbibed in the body, can unveil itself to become the Divine sole (supreme consciousness). Such knowledge and power are completely unveiled through the practice of poses faithfully, sincerely, regularly and devotionally.

The atoms existing in different matters are present in human body of the same quality, power and energy. The excess or deficiency of any element in the body causes imbalance, inequality and disorder in the body and mind are known as diseases, disorders and ailments. Poses are used to treat such disorders and ailments, which negate the ailments and cure the physical and mental disorders and diseases.

Presence of foreign matter and bodies leads to physical and mental diseases and disorders when the body tries to get rid of it. The nature has made and created the human body in such a manner, and infused it with life — performing automatic activities through four cavities of human body (head cavity, thorax cavity, abdominal cavity and pelvic cavity) that any foreign matter cannot remain in the body for long. If it remains or stays in the body the disease becomes chronic and even fatal. Diseases and disorders of mind and body are actually warnings and suggestions from the nature to clean, oust and balance it. Firstly the body and mind start their own efforts unconsciously by adopting suitable poses and postures to remove those foreign matters and bodies. If the problems are a bit difficult, human beings take help from doctors or specialists of different systems of medicine. Tantropathy is a method of treatment by Mudras, Yantras and Mantras and it certainly helps balance the five matters in the body, to energise the body and mind, to tolerate and bear the pain and suffering.

The number of poses depends on the types of forms which a body can adopt in different mental states and situations. Hence poses are in limited numbers, whereas our feelings, emotions and desires are unlimited. We will discuss here some of divine or Deva Mudras for health, fitness and happiness. Our five fingers represent the elements of five matters and with the help of these fingers of our hands we form different poses for balancing the imbalanced matters in the body. Our five fingers represent and are carriers of energies of five matters as follows:

- Angushtha (Thumb) : fire element
- Tarjani (Index finger) : air element
- Madhyama (Middle finger) : sky element
- Anamika (Ring finger) : prithivi element
- Kanishtha (Little finger) : water element

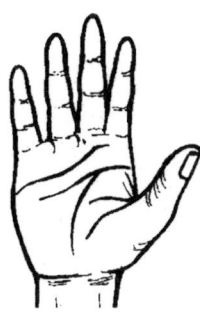

Yoga Elements

We can combine and balance five elements of our body by forming poses with fingers pressure and eye movements. We can also influence energies from these elements of matter from the universe to balance the body. We can increase or decrease the effect of various elements of the body by poses (Mudra) formed with the help of our five fingers and balance the body's elements. Some of the conventional Mudras are described here.

::::::::

SURYA MUDRA (SUN POSTURE)

Sun is the source of energy. Virtue of its energy is present in all living beings. The Sun mudra attracts energy of the Sun. It makes a person energetic. The universe is full of energy. No person can remain active without energy. As soon as content of energy is reduced in the body, inferiority complex sets in inside the person, though he may appear to be fat. The ring finger denotes earth element, whereas fire element is represented by thumb. The Sun mudra along with Sun voice enhances heat. Energy can be accumulated very fast if mudras are made by both the hands.

Method

The ring finger is placed at the base of the thumb and pressure is applied by the thumb. This is Sun mudra. The combination of the ring finger and thumb gives rise to the flow of special energy.

Sun (Surya) Mudra

Asana (Pose)

Padmasana and Siddhasana are useful in Sun mudra.

Asana

Sit comfortably on the asana. Place heel of the left leg at the vacant space between anus and penis, and then lift and place the right leg on the upper ankle of left leg. Keep the spine straight. Make Sun mudra and keep your hands steady on knees.

Duration

The Sun mudra can be continued for at least 8 minutes. If this mudra in kept for a longer period it increases the warmth. In winters, it can be kept continued for 20 minutes, but it should not be used for longer durations in summer season.

Results

- Increases the body strength.
- Energy and heat are transmitted in the whole body.
- The body gains its balance.
- Reduces weight.
- Reduces tension.
- Reduces obesity.

Effects

Thumb radiates fire element whereas ring finger radiates earth element. The earth is affected by energy. The earth element absorbs the fire element. The fire element possesses transmitting potential, whereas the earth element is the receiver.

The centre of light is situated on the forehead, on which auspicious mark (tilak) is applied with the ring finger and the thumb. The energy of ring finger and thumb activates the energy flow on the centre of light (pituitary gland), which helps develop spiritual knowledge.

Special note

According to acupressure, index points of thyroid exist at the base of the thumb. Thyroid maintains balance between the size and kind of the body. By exerting pressure on thyroid points, a balance is maintained in its outflows.

Precaution

Persons with weak bodies are advised not to do this mudra.

GYAN MUDRA (POSTURE OF KNOWLEDGE)

Knowledge is a specific characteristic of consciousness. It is the knowledge that differentiates between living and non-living things. That which possesses knowledge is living, and that lacking knowledge is non-living. The evolution of knowledge makes a person someone special out of a commoner. The following are two means of accumulation of knowledge:

- Developing the knowledge by practice.
- Availability/revelation of knowledge through exposure of awareness.

The knowledge developed through senses and mind is known as intellect-knowledge. This knowledge, when acquires the capability of making others understand it becomes 'shruta gyan' (heard knowledge). In ancient times, knowledge used to be developed by hearing. Vedas, scriptures, tripitak etc. were memorised. These were to be committed to memory only by hearing. Later, when this knowledge started getting recorded by means of signs of knowledge, this heard knowledge took the shape of scriptures and started appearing in the form of books. Collection of knowledge in book form had an added advantage. Dissemination of heard knowledge was not easy. Possession of heard knowledge was not an easy task; people had to toil hard from the childhood itself to become knowledgeable.

Able persons were appointed for imparting knowledge. By passage of time, this process of learning through hearing grew weaker. As a result, the memory also started getting weaker. The mudra, which is used for the development of memory and knowledge, is called Gyan Mudra (Knowledge posture). It is also known "Chinmaya Mudra".

Method

Keep both the hands on knees, bring together the upper tip of index finger and upper tip of thumb. Put light pressure. Keep other three fingers straight and touching each other. The shape of the hand which is formed by thumb and index finger is Gyan Mudra. Maximum use of Gayn mudra is made while meditating. Make this mudra as per the figure given below.

Gyan Mudra (Posture of knowledge)

Asana

Padmasana is the ideal asana for Gyan mudra. This mudra can also be used in Vajrasana, Sukhasana etc. Under unusual circumstances, this mudra can be used while sitting on a chair.

Method of Padmasana

Sit with outstretched legs. Bend right leg at the knee and place it on left thigh (santhl). The heel should be touching the area near the navel. Lift the left forefoot by hand and place it firmly on right thigh. Keep the heel near navel. Keep the spine and neck straight.

Duration

Normally, duration of Gyan mudra is 48 minutes. Duration may be extended as per your convenience. However, a practitioner must devote at least 15 minutes in one sitting, and for quick result one should practise regularly for 48 minutes. The mudra can be practised during meditation or during activities that do not require use of index finger and thumb.

Results

- Develops knowledge.
- Develops memory.
- Changes the behaviour/attitudes of obstinacy, irritation, instability, anger, impatience, and restlessness, which are pacified.
- Mind becomes calm and cheerful.
- Increases concentration; successful in area of work.
- Easy feeling towards studies.
- Nerves of brain get stronger.
- Headache and insomnia are cured.

Special note

The acupressure therapy considers relationship between finger-tips and brain. Exertion of pressure on these points relieves headache and develops faculties of mind. The spot near upper tip of thumb is the centre of pituitary and pineal glands. Pituitary is master gland. These glands play an important role in bodily balance and evolution of personality. Pressing of these glands leads of emergence of the feelings of friendship, compassion, fearlessness, stability, sincerity etc.; while maintaining Gyan mudra, worshipping and meditating with concentration on yellow colour on forehead not only increases appropriate opportunity of development of intellect but also strengthens the nervous system, which makes a reader free from lethargy, drowsiness and sleepiness.

Precautions

Persons desiring development of knowledge should avoid sour and spicy food. Excessive hot and cold drinks are also prohibited. Use of pan masala, betelnut, chutaki, tobacco etc. should also be avoided.

Legs should not be shaken unnecessarily while sitting on a table, chair or stool. Speaking ill of others, jealousy and hatred should be avoided. Knowledge and knowledgeable persons both should not be disrespected and neglected. One should not be egoistic about one's knowledge. It is important to keep the knowledge and the knowledgeable persons in high esteem, and the latter should be dealt with politely for getting knowledge. This makes the knowledge perfect.

VAYU MUDRA (AIR POSTURE)

A person can live without food for a few months, can also stay alive for a few days without water, but without air it is impossible to live even for a few minutes. Thus, the importance of air in our lives can well be understood. The Ayurveda believes that balance of wind (vata), bile (pitta) and phlegm (kuff) keeps the body healthy. Imbalance of these elements leads to disorders and diseases in the body. So long air is maintained evenly in the body, the latter remains healthy. Unbalanced air causes ill health. As such, balance of air is necessary for health and tranquility of the body. The practitioners of Ayurveda claim that by pulse examination balance or imbalance of the air can be detected. As per Ayurveda there are 25 types of air in the body. Its disorder is quite frightening. Disorder in the body worries the patient. Air symbolises unsteadiness. Its disorder enhances the unsteadiness of mind. Vayu mudra is used for making the mind steady. It is a useful discovery of the sages.

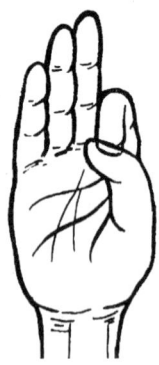

Vayu Mudra (Air posture)

Method

Bent fore-finger (tarjani) is placed at the base of the thumb. In this Vayu Mudra the remaining three fingers are kept straight. See the figure given here for guidance.

Asana

Stay with bent (tarjani) knee in Vajrasana with Vayu mudra. Keep spine straight. Keep thumbs of both feet touching each other. Heels should also be in close proximity. It is useful to keep buttocks on heels. Persons who suffer from indigestion and gastric disorders, should use this mudra along with the asana for 5 minutes after meals.

Results

Use of Vayu mudra reduces the unsteadiness of mind. The vital air starts flowing in Sushumna, one of the major nerves that plays an important role in the achievement of supreme bliss.

- The irate wind is pacified.
- A number of diseases like vibrated wind, gout, sciatica, gastric pain and paralysis get cured.
- Body pain due to the wind is cured.
- Knees and joint pain are alleviated. Pain in spinal column, waist and other parts of the body also get removed gradually.
- Pain in the neck can also be removed by it.

Special note

As per acupressure therapy, the index finger contains pressure points for spine. By exerting pressure on these points, disorders of spine are removed and the spine gets stronger. The base of the thumb, where fore finger is placed, has harmonising points for important part of the throat. Pressure on these points keeps whole of the body balanced and healthy. As a result personality acquires elegance. Qualities like virility, efficiency etc. develop.

Precautions

- In view of alleviation of body pain, one tries to repeat the mudras several times, but the time limit must be kept in mind.
- With the usage of Vayu mudra, the Vayu element in the body fluctuates. The use of the mudra should be increased or decreased only after assessment of its impact on the body.
- The use of mudra should be discontinued when the pain subsides or the wind gets even.

::::::::

AKASH MUDRA (SKY POSTURE)

The sky has an attribute — recess or space. Another attribute is sound. Sound is regarded as the eternal spirit. Sound travels in waves, which are scattered in the sky. By catching the sound waves, we are able to hear these on radio. As the sky provides space outside, so is the sky spreads inside. The lack or excess of elements in the sky outside leads to imbalance.

The third attribute of the sky is vacuum or nothingness. This is the attribute that fills the sky. The sky can be filled only when it has nothing. How can already filled sky be filled? The yoga helps practise meditation in the inner space. Emotions get purified when one concentrates in the heart. The middle finger and the heart are interrelated.

Method

When upper tip of the thumb is touched with the front portion of the middle finger, Akash mudra is formed. Form the mudra as per the figure given here.

Akash Mudra (Sky posture)

Asana

Practice of Akash mudra in Vajrasana is most powerful. This mudra may also be used in other asanas of meditation. For the method of asana follow the procedure for Vayu mudra.

Duration

Do not practice for more than 16 minutes at one sitting. It may be used for 48 minutes in three sittings. As per Jain system, duration of 'Antarmuhurta' has been prescribed for all kinds of exercises. For any ritual for which no duration has been fixed, the 'Antarmuhurta' is 2 to 48 minutes. However, its normal duration is 48 minutes.

Results

- The "Akash mudra" removes emptiness.
- The hearing faculty is improved.
- Disorders related to ear e.g. running of the ear, or pain in the ear, get cured.
- Helps in curing heart disease and related disorders.
- Strengthens bones.

Special note

As per acupressure therapy, the middle finger also contains points of sinus. By pressing these points, cold and sinus get cured. The astrology considers this finger to be representative of Shani (Saturn). Union of fire and Saturn elements leads to evolution of spiritual power. While worshipping, hands are kept near the heart. It is the middle finger that pushes the beads of rosary for prosperity and glory. With 'Akash mudra' person becomes fearless. The practice of "Abhaya mudra" produces scintillating power and awakening. It is desirable to maintain patience during the practice of Akash mudra. It is only through this mudra that a person attains the desired goal.

Precautions

- Hands are not to be kept reserved after adopting the mudra.
- Do not practice 'Akash mudra' while walking.
- Do not practice this mudra while taking meals.

PRITHVI MUDRA (EARTH POSTURE)

The earth element is also a constituent in the formation of the body. It is a gross element, which has more weight content. By Prithvi mudra, the earth element is balanced. The earth is a fundamental element, which helps evolution of life. It is like a mother to living beings. The earth has endurance capacity. The Jain scriptures exhort ascetics to make themselves like earth. 'Prithvi same muni hveja'. The Prithvi mudra is useful for developing the quality of steadiness. A steadfast person can be forebearing. The earth tolerates all types of circumstances. Whatever be the conditions — winter, summer or rains — the earth remains balanced. Not only this, the earth forgives all those who defile it and pollute the environment. The solid element, present in the body, is a part of the earth. We take earth element only from the food we eat. The deficiency of earth element weakens the body. The Prithvi mudra is useful for the development of earth element in the body. The ring finger, which denotes the earth element, is used in worshipping and applying auspicious mark (tilak).

Prithvi Mudra (Earth posture)

Method

Ring finger is adjacent to the little finger. When the front tip of the ring finger is touched to the upper tip of the thumb, 'Prithvi mudra' is formed. The remaining fingers are kept straight. See this figure for guidance.

Asana

Vajrasana is the best suited asana for "Prithvi mudra". But this mudra can also be practiced in "Sukhasana" and meditational asanas. For method of this asana, please refer to Vayu mudra.

Duration

For making the body balanced and well-shaped, "Prithvi mudra" can be practiced for 24 minutes.

Effects

- The body becomes strong and healthy.
- It develops lustre and glow.
- Increases happiness, magnanimity and thoughtfulness.
- The body and mind feel lightness.
- The virtue of ignorance (Tamoguna) appear. Feeling of detachment sets in, and digestion process improves.

Special

As per acupressure therapy, the pressure points of sinus remove the disorders related to cold and catarrh.

- This mudra makes the body stronger and healthier.

- Feeling of freshness and happiness is experienced.
- Vitality is developed.

Person with obesity should use Prithvi mudra. It cures dumbness.

Precautions

Since the Prithvi element increases weight and strength, it is advisable to use this mudra not more than required.

VARUN MUDRA (WATER POSTURE)

Varun means water. Water is life. Like air, water is vital for life. A person can live without food for a few months, but it is difficult to stay alive without water for more than a few days. Fluidity is the characteristic attributed to water. The water not only helps in liquidising the food, but it also creates various elements. Deficiency of water element in the body increases dryness and makes the body cells dry, which then become inactive. In the absence of water element neither the flow of vital air, nor its circulation can be settled. The water element provides coolness and activity.

Method

The little finger (Kanishtha) symbolises water element. For joining the water element and fire element, front tips of little finger and of thumb are joined to make "Varun mudra".

Varun Mudra (Water posture)

Asana

Limited practice in winter is recommended. In all other seasons, practice it at least for 24 minutes. Complete duration is of 48 minutes. The duration may be fixed according to the balance of body elements.

Results

- The dryness of the body disappears.
- The glow and smoothness of the body increases.
- The skin becomes glossy and soft.
- Skin ailments disappear.
- Blood disorders disappear.
- Youthfulness remains for a longer period, old age is delayed.
- This mudra quenches the thirst.

Special note

As per acupressure therapy, the little finger of left hand represents left portion of the body. Similarly, the little finger of right hand is symbolic of right portion. The little fingers, affecting the left and right parts of the body, are influenced by fire element. By exerting pressures on both the fingers, the left and right portions of the body become healthy and strong. Disorders are removed. By massaging the little finger with thumb, while practising this posture, the energy is balanced. The state of unconsciousness ends. It shows spectacular results in sudden accidents.

Precautions

Persons with cold or phlegmatic tendency should not practice Varun mudra for a long period and without proper guidance.

APAAN MUDRA (FLATUS POSTURE)

The vital air is mainly present in whole of the body. This vital air carries different activities in different parts and areas of the body. As such, these have been given different names e.g. pran, apaan, samaan, udaan and vyan. This air group works separately at five major centres.

The place of vital air is situated mainly in the heart at bliss point (Anaahad Chakra). The vital air helps in breathing, digesting the food, segregating juices of food into different units, making juices from the food and formation of other metals. The apaan is situated in health centre and energy centre, which are known as Swadhi Sthan Chakra and Muladhar Chakra in the Yoga. Its place is inside arms up to penis.

Functions of apaan include expelling urine, semen, menstruation and foetus. It supports dynamic activities like sleeping, sitting, getting up, walking etc. Disposal is as much essential for life as acquisition is. It would be very

Apaan Mudra

difficult for a person to stay alive even for a day if his body has only acquisition systems and no arrangement for disposal. Disposal helps in purifying the body. If there is a breakdown of the disposal systems of the body for two or three days, whole of the body would stink and it would be difficult for a person to remain healthy. Apaan mudra purifies impurities and filth.

Method

By joining tips of middle and ring fingers and thumb and putting pressure, Apaan mudra is formed. Index and little fingers are to be kept straight.

Asana

Utkatasan is most useful for this mudra. However, it can be used in any of the meditational asanas, e.g. Sukhasana.

Duration

This should be repeated thrice for duration of 16 minutes each time. The practice for 48 minutes enables transformation to the height of realisation. Pran and apaan, both are important for the body. The ultimate objective of yoga is to make pran as well as apaan even. Their union brings stability to mind and leads to intense meditation.

Results

- Body and nerves are purified.
- The body disposes off the faeces and other defects and the body attains purity.
- Constipation is rectified. It is quite useful for piles.
- Improves the potential of various parts of abdomen.

- Pacifies air disorder and diabetes.
- Blockage in urinary tract and disorders of kidneys are removed.
- Tooth disorders and pain get alleviated.
- Removes the heat of the body, as it results in sweating.
- Heart becomes stronger.

Special note

As per acupressure, its pressure points remove the diseases related to bronchial tube and stomach, as well as urinary disorders.

Both the hands are to be used for this mudra. It helps in getting complete benefit. If one hand is busy in some other work, it can be carried on with the other hand. This mudra is most beneficial when carried out with both the hands, but is less beneficial with one hand. With the union of pran and apaan, the practitioner Sadhaka becomes 'Urdhvareta'.

Precautions

This mudra may lead to increased discharge of urine. There is no need to worry about this.

PRAN MUDRA (VITAL AIR POSTURE)

The vital air (pran vayu) enters the lungs along with breath. In turn, lungs mix it with blood and send it to the heart. Action of combustion starts when glucose present in cells and vital air (oxygen) present in blood come into contact, which produces energy. The pranacharya have identified five types of air in the body — pran, apaan, samaan, udaan and vyaan. They are spread in various parts of the body.

It is the pran that energises the body. Excess or deficiency of pran creates imbalance. Pran mudra is used to strike the balance of pran and keep the body energetic.

Method

The mudra which is created by joining the tips of little finger (water element) and ring finger (earth element) with the thumb (fire element) is known as Pran mudra. It is a very powerful mudra.

Pran mudra (Vital Air Posture)

Asana

Padmasana or Siddhasana makes the vital energy intense. By keeping the spine straight, the vital energy becomes active and vertically inclined.

Duration

A duration of 48 minutes is considered complete for systematising the vital air. Since it may not be possible to practice this mudra for a complete duration at a stretch, it may be staggered into two or three phases. To start with, practice it for 16 minutes and gradually consummate it to the desired duration.

Results

- The deficiency of vital energy can be removed and it is then gradually increased by Pran mudra. It strengthens bronchial tube.
- Weakness of body, disturbance of mind and rigidness of feeling are removed.
- Removes eye disorders and increases sight.
- Makes a man dignified.
- Makes a man Urdhvareta.
- Person comes across subtle elements and starts merging with the Eternal Soul.
- Develops concentration.
- The Pran mudra energises the whole of the body. It is helpful in regenerating the energy lost due to paralysis.

Precautions

Pran is energy. It is power. It becomes virtuous with proper use of senses, mind and emotions. Otherwise it can lead senses towards attachment, mind to disturbance and emotions to perversion. As such efforts should continue towards balanced adjustment for the development of vital energy produced by Pran mudra, otherwise the increasing energy with body may channelise itself towards downfall instead of upward development.

Special note

Pran mudra has simultaneous union of three elements: water, earth and fire. All these three elements come into contact and lead to chemical transformation in the body, which helps in balanced development of the personality. The Pran mudra is specially useful in meditational yoga e.g. fast. It helps in natural and easy consummation of meditation.

::::::::

ANGUSHTHA MUDRA (THUMB POSTURE)

Angushtha mudra is also called Linga mudra (Phallus posture). Thumb is a symbol of masculinity. It helps in increasing dynamism in a person. It increases heat. Persons with bilious temperament should practice this mudra under the guidance of able and experienced person, otherwise the increasing bilious wrath may lead to increase in acidity in the body. Moreover, due to excessive heat, all these ailments like pain, giddiness, dryness of throat and increased burning sensation in the body may further increase. This mudra can be used during winter season. It removes phlegmatic disorders. Chronic cold is easily cured. It burns unwanted calories in the body, thus reducing obesity.

Method

For making Angushtha mudra, fingers of both the hands are interlocked, and the left thumb is kept straight while the palms are pressed against each other; pressure is also exerted on back portion by fingers. Right thumb is

Angushtha Mudra (Thumb Posture)

to be placed at the base of left thumb and pressure is to be applied. For the first time left thumb is kept straight, and the second time pressure may be applied at the base of right thumb. Angushtha (Linga) mudra is accomplished through both the ways.

Asana

Padmasana and Ardha Padmasana are useful asanas for Linga mudra. Those not successful in these asanas may use this mudra in Sukhasana and Vajrasana.

Duration

The Angushtha mudra can be practiced early in the morning or on cool nights. It can be practised for 48 minutes at a stretch or in three phases of 16 minutes each.

Results

- Pacifies cough.
- Cures asthma and cold.
- Cures sinus and paralysis.

Special note

As per acupressure therapy, practice of the mudra gives strength to the body. Pressure on rear portion of the palm removes disorders present in the body.

Precautions

Persons with bilious temperament should not use this mudra for longer period. Persons with abdomen tumour are forbidden to practise this mudra.

SURABHI MUDRA (FRAGRANCE POSTURE)

Surabhi mudra is also called Dhenu mudra. As per Indian system, dhenu means cow. It symbolises virtue (Satvikata) and excellence. The other meaning of surabhi, as per dictionary, is Kamadhenu (the special cow) which gives desired boons. Similarly, with Surabhi mudra a person acquires the desired power. While making Surabhi mudra, fingers take the shape of udders of a cow. Milk is obtained from the udders of cow, which gives strength to the body. Similarly, the Surabhi mudra makes the body balanced and strong.

According to Ayurveda, by maintaining balance between wind (vata), bile (pitta) and phlegm (kuff), body remains healthy. Imbalance is the source of diseases. Surabhi mudra balances the wind, bile and phlegm. It makes the body healthy. The body of man is physical, it is atomic. Proper combination of atomic energy makes the body strong. Improper combination weakens the body. Balance of all the five elements in body results in health,

Surabhi Mudra

otherwise problems arise. Fingers of the hand represent all the five elements. The balanced order of five elements in the body leads to development. Surabhi mudra strikes balance in all the five elements.

Method

Join the front tips of fingers of both the hands with each other. Make the left forefinger touch the middle finger of right hand. Let the right hand forefinger touch the middle finger of left hand. Similarly, join the ring finger of left hand with little finger of right hand and the little finger of left hand with ring finger of right hand. Thumbs will be left free. When fingers are put downward, the shape of fingers looks like udders of cow. Thus it is called Surabhi mudra (Dhenu mudra).

Asana

Utkatasana is best suited for Surabhi mudra. If there is a difficulty in this asana, this mudra may be practiced in Vajrasana or Sukhasana.

Method for Utkatasana

The pose of sitting straight on soles of the feet is known as Utkatasana.

Duration

To start with, practice it for 8 minutes. After practising it for a week, increase the duration to 16 minutes. Finally this mudra may be practiced up to 48 minutes duration. If it is not possible to do it at a stretch, the duration of 48 minutes may be divided into three sittings.

Results

- Navel centre becomes healthy.
- Helps in yoga practice.
- Pacifies urinary diseases.
- Makes body healthy and strong.
- Makes digestive system healthy.
- Cures abdomen-related diseases.
- Strikes balance in flows of gland system.
- Improves purity of mind.

Special note

In Surabhi mudra air element meets the sky element and earth element meets the water element but fire element (thumb) remains free. The union of air and sky elements stabilises the Brahmand Chakra. Like Brahmand Chakra, the navel chakra of the body also becomes healthy and steady. Creative power is developed by the union of water and earth of the chakras.

In Surabhi mudra several forms are developed with the union of five elements. This has varied results. Methods and results of these are described separately.

Water Surabhi

The little finger represents water element. In Surabhi mudra the thumb is placed at the base of little finger, which starts alleviating bilious problems and diseases. It helps in making kidneys healthy and it rectifies urinary disorders. It is useful for persons with bilious temperament.

Earth Surabhi

The ring finger symbolises earth element. By placing

the thumb at the base of ring finger, Surabhi mudra is accomplished. The Earth mudra alleviates diseases related to abdomen. It keeps the digestive system in order. The Earth mudra makes the body powerful. It removes inertia and heaviness.

Sky Surabhi

The middle finger is representative of sky element. This is also called Shunya mudra. Characteristics of emptiness and sound are attributed to sky. This mudra leads to coordination of sounds. The inner sky gets rid of noise. An atmosphere of tranquility is created. Sound of 'naad' appears. The feeling of 'Anaahad naad' is easily reached through this mudra.

Air Surabhi

In Surabhi mudra when fire element is joined with the ring finger of air element, the development of air element begins. It removes various gastric disorders. These gastric disorders are not revealed by medical examinations. A person starts feeling serenity immediately with the use of Vayu mudra. It increases the steadiness of mind. It is especially useful for those engaged in meditation and worship.

Precautions

Surabhi mudra should be used only after considering all aspects. If only gastric disorder is there, the five elements can be made to touch the base of air-element finger, which pacifies gastric disorders.

Self practitioner must keep in mind his body temperaments. For persons with phlegm temperament the fire element pacifies the phlegm, but it also reduces the water element. It is therefore suggested to use this mudra for a shorter duration.

Surabhi Mudra

It is a multi-dimensional mudra. As such it has some opposing results. The fire element mudra is useful for pacifying gas. But simultaneously it increases heat also.

MRIGI MUDRA (ANTELOPE POSTURE)

Mrigi mudra is symbolic of deer. Deer is a very innocent creature. Among vegetarians deer is one of the animals that can be seen leaping in hermitage. Hide of deer is used by sages as their seats. The Mrigi mudra is one of the mudras that are used during worship, adoration, recitation of hymns and meditation rituals. For its simplicity, virtuousness and naturalness, this mudra is called Mrigi mudra, whose formation looks like a fawn.

Method

The Mrigi mudra is formed by touching the middle portions of ring and middle fingers with the front part of the thumb. Index and little fingers are kept straight. The shape looks like the mouth of a deer. As such it is called "Mrigi mudra".

Mrigi Mudra (Antelope Posture)

Asana

Asanas such as Sukhasana and Utkatasana used during worship enhance its effectiveness.

Duration

This mudra is used at the time of meditation, worship,

rituals etc. This mudra is formed in accordance with the number of repetitions of hymns (Japa). Usually, it takes 8 to 10 minutes in completing a hymn or rosary for 108 times. Normally, flow of feeling continues for a maximum of 48 minutes. As such this mudra may be extended up to 48 minutes.

Special note

The Mrigi mudra represents simplicity and straightness. A straight person alone can undertake religious worship with ease. A deity is always influenced by simplicity and straightess. Mudras are mirrors of feelings. Mudras may influence the exterior atmosphere, which influences the mudra. The stage of mudras leads to evolution of awakening.

As per acupressure therapy, these fingers contain tooth and sinus points, which alleviate disorders related to cold and give relief to toothache. The pressure exerted with the thumb-tip reduces the headache and tension due to cold.

Results

- Evolves straightness.
- Stabilises the mind.
- Purifies feelings.
- Useful in epilepsy.

Precaution

Avoid feelings becoming mutilated or passionate because under such conditions heat may generate.

HANSI MUDRA (LAUGHTER POSTURE)

Laughter is a symbol for wisdom. It is a means of expression of person's wisdom. "Hansi mudra" is used for nutritive activities. It leads it all-round prosperity.

Method

Tips of all but little finger are pressed by the front tip of the thumb, for forming this mudra.

Hansi Mudra

Asana

Sukhasana or Utkatasana may be used.

Duration

To start with it can be used for 8 minutes and then this duration can be extended to 48 minutes.

Results

- Develops wisdom.
- Increases lightness.
- Completeness is reached.

Special note

This mudra leads to the development of regality.

Precaution

Recitation of hymns etc. is forbidden in this mudra.

SHANKH MUDRA (SHELL POSTURE)

The conch is considered to be an auspicious object in the Indian system. It is used for worshipping the God. Normally the conch has been making auspicious sounds throughout man's journey form birth to salvation. The acharyas analysing the word Shankh say that which leads to welfare is known as Shankh. It is with the sounding of conch that the doors of temples are opened. Our lives are most affected by sound. The sound waves prevent calamities and also help in attaining the desired goals.

Method

Place firmly the left-hand thumb on the right palm and close the fist. Let the right-hand thumb touch the remaining fingers. Thus all the four fingers touch the fire element. This mudra leads the hand in conch shape. Thus it is called "Shankh mudra". The opening between fingers and thumb at the upper side is like the mouth of the conch. If

Shankh Mudra (Conch Posture)

you try to blow through this portion, as you blow a sound similar to that provided by a conch is generated. This mudra can also be formed by changing hands.

Asana

This mudra can be used properly in Ukduasana or Sampadasana. It may also be practiced in Sukhasana and Vajrasana.

Duration

Initially it may be practiced for 16 minutes, but may be continued gradually for 48 minutes.

Results

- Removes speech disorders. Gives sweetness to voice.
- Disorders related to tonsil and throat get removed.
- It keeps navel centre in order, making person healthy.
- Alleviates abdomen disorders. Improves digestive system.

Special note

German scientists experimented on conch sound and found that diseases like those of thyroid, plague, cholera etc. do not influence atmosphere and it helps in alleviating these diseases and other disorders. The body elements feel change by formation of Shankh mudra. This balance of elements destroys harmful elements, and simultaneously helps in creation of useful elements. The Shankh mudra shape makes all five elements join in fire element, which leads to avoidance and refinement of their disorders.

Precautions

As per acupressure therapy, by pressing the thumb thyroid gland is influenced. To keep its hormones balanced, special care is required. If the body starts getting weaker or fatter, this mudra should be stopped. The lower position of the thumb represents the front of Venus. If this position of Venus is reddish or pain free, it may be concluded that the person is healthy.

Other types of Shankh mudra

In the other types of Shankh mudra, all the eight fingers of both the hands are entangled with each other, and when both the thumbs are pressed by forefingers, the upper portion of thumbs bulges out. The opening between both, when blown, produces conch like sound. This may be practiced through Vajrasana.

PANKAJ MUDRA (LOTUS POSTURE)

As per Indian system, lotus is a symbol of purity. Like a lotus, which remains detached from the mud in which it blooms, a sage remains detached from the mud of attachment, while continuing his meditation.

Method

By keeping the fingers like lotus, the Pankaj mudra is formed. In this mudra both the thumbs and little fingers touch each other. This mudra develops the fire and water elements and refines those elements. Like the lotus which blooms at sunrise, the fire element makes the inner lotus bloom. At night, like the blooming of lotus under moonlight the water element also brightens the face (Chandra Kamal). The remaining fingers face each other, which naturally leads to transition of their virtues, leading to development of the capability to provide vital energy to others.

Pankaj Mudra (Lotus Posture)

Asana

Use of Pankaj mudra in Padmasana or Sampada Asana gives spontaneous results.

Duration

Initially use it for 16 minutes. The complete practice takes 48 minutes. If it is not possible to do it at a stretch, stagger the process in three phases.

Result

- ☞ Water and fire elements in the body get balanced. Makes the behaviour gentle.
- ☞ Enhances the beauty of the body.
- ☞ Makes the nerve system stronger.
- ☞ Removes blood disorders.
- ☞ Makes the spine healthy.
- ☞ Pacifies fever.
- ☞ Cures abdominal tumour.

Special note

During meditation in Pankaj mudra, the virtue of detachment gets enhanced. Lotus is considered to be a symbol of detachment and purity.

Precautions

Restricted use of Pankaj mudra in winters is recommended, otherwise it may lead to increase in phlegm. The lotus does not develop fully under condition of asthmatic and cough disorders.

TANTROPATHY

ANUSHASAN MUDRA (DISCIPLINE POSTURE)

Discipline is the vital element of meditation. Without discipline, meditation is not successful. The practitioner can maintain discipline through his own discretion. He must remain under the discipline of the Guru (teacher), so long as his wisdom does not become awakened and he is not enlightened.

Method

For Anushasan mudra, keep the index finger straight. Join the remaining three fingers with the thumb. The mudra so formed is called Anushasan mudra.

Anushasan Mudra (Discipline Posture)

Asana

This mudra may be used in Padmasana and Sukhasana. Sampadasana is also suitable for this mudra.

Duration

Start with 8 minutes daily. Increase by a minute per day for a month.

Results

- ☞ Develops discipline.
- ☞ Increases leadership quality.
- ☞ Increases efficiency.
- ☞ It is a primordial formula for success.

Special note

As per acupressure therapy, it influences spinal column. Person experiences virility within himself.

Precaution

Do not continue for a longer period at a stretch.

SAMANVAY MUDRA
(CO-ORDINATION POSTURE)

By joining all the fingers, coordination of five elements is established. This is called Samanvay mudra. By joining fingers and thumb, the posture looks like the snout of a pig. As such it is called "Shukari mudra" also. This mudra is also used in tantrik rituals of 'Maaran' (mantra for killing the adversary) and "Uchchatan" (causing to quit one's occupation by means of magical incantation). It is considered to be a strong mudra in the Yoga. The applications of mantra sankalpa (resolve) in Shukari mudra are undoubtedly successful.

Method

A hollow space is formed in the palm by joining fingers and the thumb. This makes all the fire elements of water, earth, sky, wind and fire combined. Since it takes the form of the snout of a pig, it is called Shukari mudra.

Samanvay Mudra (Co-ordination Posture)

Asana

Sukhasana and Padmasana are appropriate for this mudra.

Duration

In accordance with recitation and rituals, the duration of 8 minutes may be increased to 48 minutes.

Results

- ☞ The feeling of coordination is enhanced.
- ☞ Develops strength.
- ☞ Balances the elements.
- ☞ Prevents calamities.

Special note

As per acupressure therapy, by joining finger and thumb tips, pressure is exerted on mind and pituitary gland, which results in removal of their disorders. The vedic scriptures relate an instance where Lord Vishnu, incarnated as a pig, performed a heroic deed of retrieval of the earth by its teeth. By performing rituals in this mudra, the power appears. Efforts are successful.

Precaution

Do not use this mudra for a long duration because balance of power is desirable, but excess of power can create havoc. As such maintenance of balance is of utmost importance.

VEETRAG MUDRA (DISPASSIONATE POSTURE)

This is the purest form of enlightenment, which is realised or experienced through knowledge. The knowledge is defiled by imposition of attachment and detachment. It does not remain pure and it leads to bonds. The Veetrag mudra is useful in maintaing freedom from bondage. For preparation of observational meditation, this mudra is used following the asana. "Mudra is the mirror of feeling, feeling is a mirror of mudra." This principle is used to practise the Veetrag mudra. Its use helps in gradual development of Veetrag feelings.

Method

The left palm will stay near navel. Right palm will be kept over it. Thumbs will remain on each other.

Veetrag Mudra

Asana

Though Padmasana is the best suited asana for Veetrag mudra, it can be practised in Sukhasana and Vajrasana also.

Duration

The Veetrag mudra is a mudra of meditation, for which it is best suited. It may be practised from 1 minute to 45 minutes.

Results

- Develops Veetrag (dispassionate) feeling.
- Makes the energy move upward.
- Develops stability.
- Balances energy.
- Leads to equation among elements.

Special note

Veetrag is a mudra for meditation. Most of the idols and Lord Tirthankars are in Veetrag mudra. It is a useful and easy mudra. In this mudra both the hands are touched forming circle of power, which may lead a person to the depths of meditation. The memory of veetrag easily leads to the development of veetrag feelings. The body possesses negative and positive both types of electric charges. By joining of both the hands, the Veetrag mudra is formed easily. This attracts a person towards Veetrag feelings. This mudra is imbibed with stability and impartiality.

CHAPTER 2

- How do techniques of
  tantropathy work?...............................82

HOW DO TECHNIQUES OF TANTROPATHY WORK?

The age-old Indian cult tantra is the way of "Purusharth Path" (all-round development of human personality). Usually the practice of tantrik techniques is used for spiritual development, and the practitioners develop their mental faculties and physical health by this process. This is the reason that a yogi or tantrik is physically fit, mentally balanced and spiritually evolved. Spirituality is no religion, which is based on dogmas, but is a scientific way of sociability. It helps converting ourselves to social self and ultimately merging to supreme sense (consciousness). There is a common saying in India: "Himmate mard, marde khuda", meaning that if you are courageous enough (physically fit, mentally balanced, emotionally stable and spiritually evoled), you are the person to attain consciousness. Hence techniques of tantropathy contribute to health and peace of mind basically and increase the life force unlimitedly, though these are not explained scientifically. But modern researches are slowly uncovering the mechanics of Tantra-yoga and explaining the terms that can be clearly understood.

A person's mental and physical health depends on brain and body chemicals. Regular practice of the techniques of tantropahty, actually alters the brain chemistry. It slows down the action of the sympathetic nervous system in practical terms. Your body does not get flooded with stress. Ageing process is a natural phenomenon, which cannot be stopped. However, we can slow it down with the help of these techniques. Endocrine glands of our body control our growth. These glands are (a) thyroid, (b) pituitary, (c) thymus and (d) some sexual glands.

The pituitary glands control the growth of bones. When a child is born, his thymus glands are very large, but they start shrinking after the age of 13-14 years. At that stage sex glands start controlling the growth of body. The body attains full maturity at the age of 20-22 years and after that the growth stops. The glands responsible for physical growth, become less active after this age and we start ageing. But in tantropathy 'growing up' does not matter, what matters is 'climbing up'. Please keep stress at bay.

1. The principle behind the techniques of tantropathy is that we have four major cavities in our body — head cavity, thorax cavity, abdominal cavity and pelvic cavity — and we have to take proper care of the life-running installations (organs provided in these cavities by the nature). Techniques of tantropathy lead to a series of complex therapeutic actions that flush out toxins from every cell of the body. Once the morbidity caused by the toxins in every cell are eliminated, the body's response to the palliative therapy is improved unexpectedly. 'Isht Pranam' is one of the techniques of tantropathy from which we start; it will help open the channel of the body and mind to facilitate the treatment of the particular disease of a specified system of the body. We also advise to follow daily routine and to keep daily scheduled technique developed in tantropathy constant. Our body has more than 100 biological rhythms, that cycle every 24 hours (circadian rhythms), which modify our body functions such

as heart rate, hormone level, temperature, pain threshold and body temperature. Our daily schedule from visiting toilet to exercising and sleeping soundly greatly inflames our body and mind and our brain orders more cells to set these rhythms without side influence.

2. Therapeutic techniques of tantropathy consist of tantrik poses, mantra and yantra along with yogic postures in unity, continuity, and rhythmic manner. The detoxification techniques are to be practiced by all age groups of persons (gents and ladies) and by those who want a well-built body and disciplined life style. It demands total involvement of body concentration at the time of practice due to its rhythmical, systematic and continuing nature. Regular practice of these techniques also improves the functioning of parasympathetic system, which controls our ability to relax and alter the brain chemistry. Maha Mrityunjaya technique is unique for this. Our advice is that you need not worry for results but to be careful for its regularity.

Chakra Shodhan Bhedan technique (Maha Mrityunjaya Mudra) is very much successful in treating ailments like arthritis, gout, spondilitis, sciatica and other rheumatic diseases and paralysis. Migraine, sinusitis and other psycho-somatic diseases are also cured by this technique. Patients have to take special tantric diet, including 'Amritanna' (germinated gram, pea, soyabean, mung etc.) when they perform Chakra-Shodhan-Bhedan, simple Pranayam and Dharna and special type of cathartic meditation. There is an effective cathartic element in energy culture of the world, and tantropathy has chosen a few of the elements specially from Indian culture for this purpose. Actually, a person's mental and physical health depends on brain chemistry, and the practice of the technique of tantropathy alters that if required or strengthened. Practitioners should take relevant tantric herbs and minerals as lemon juice, honey, mint leaves, tulsi leaves with water orally and focus auto-vision (Bhut Shuddhi, Sharir Shuddhi and Mann Shuddhi). You will feel relaxed and rejuvenated daily.

Due to pollution additives in our food and anti bodies we consume, our bodies get clogged with substances that cause health problems. It involves a series of complex therapeutic actions that flush out toxins from every cell of the body, once the morbidity caused by the toxins is eliminated. Techniques are designed specially for physical, mental and spiritual discipline. When you are doing practice, your mind becomes alert because you think not only of your own specific part of the body but of the entire life running systems. This is dharna process. Tantra says, "without perfecting ourself in Dharna, Dhyan becomes tiresome job." Techniques of tantropathy are just and spiritual sport to play with oneself of similar or higher standard, and health, fitness and happiness comes automatically.

What is found in universe, is within our body. Our body is a mini universe. Fire, water, air weather and earth are the five elements found in this universe. Human being is also composed of these elements and if the system becomes unbalanced, we feel physically and mentally ill. Tantra says our five fingers represent these five elements, and attract the elements if proper mudras of these elements are formed. Our thumb represents fire (Agni), index (tarjani) represents air (Vayu), middle finger (madhyama) represents space (Akash), ring finger (anamika) represents earth (Prithvi) and little finger (kanishtha) represents water (Jal). If these elements are balanced in our body, we will be fit and healthy but we suffer corresponding illness if these are imbalanced. Finger postures have special significance in tantra which are called Yoga mudra, Deva mudra and Gyan-Dhyan mudra. If Yoga mudra is performed on meditative postures, it is called "Gyan-Dhyan mudra", and if it is done with other postures and poses, it is called Deva mudra. Yoga mudra done with meditative postures is easy to practice and can be performed at any time and at any place twice a day regularly, preferably during morning and evening. In the beginning only 5 minutes are sufficient. (For detailed information please see the first chapter.)

3. Techniques of tantropathy are so designed that they serve the purpose of the proportionate combined effect on body and cosmic effect on mind. These are best suited for even weight watchers and obese. Researchers have found that those who did a combination of aerobic and anaerobic exercises for 30 minutes, even thrice a week, lost twice as much weight as those who confined themselves to 30 minutes of aerobic exercises alone three times a day. The reason behind this is that techniques of tantropathy build muscles by protecting even capillaries, which consume energy and fat equally. Even while you are resting, more fat is burnt by doing regular exercises. If Tandava Nritya technique is practiced even for 3 to 5 minutes along with "Isht Pranam" for 15 minutes, it can do miracle better than aerobic and anaerobic exercises.

4. Our behaviour is controlled by the chemical transmitter system — secreting neurons of the brain in melatonin vs serotonin process. Serotonin secreting neurons of our brain spread out their fibres to suppress the activity of reticulum and brain in darkness. Thus the system promotes sleep. But melatonin-secreting neurons of our brain spread out their fibres to arouse reaction in light and myelin (a thicker insulation) is produced. Researchers have found that after concentration of light for a few minutes with certain divine poses, myelin is produced in sufficient quantity. Nirmimekh Varjan technique of tantropathy with certain postures and poses can produce sufficient melatonin and myelin. It can develop even extra-sensory perception on regular and timely practice of this technique. Tantra says, Pitri yagya should be performed with prescribed offering poses (Arpanatmak mudras) after taking bath in light without wiping the body with a towel in the morning and evening, and it will increase intelligence, memory and extra-sensory perception. It also regulates the cardio-vascular system of the body.

5. We know that our brain is the seat of thought, memory, emotions and above all intelligence. It is a well known fact that an hour of active, disturbed mind can trigger off a stress reaction in the body, raise blood pressure, lead to pounding of heart, tenses muscles and throws powerful negative thoughts, which can leave a person drained of physical and mental energy. Working whole-heartedly is the unique aspect of personality but to become workaholic is the tragedy for the human being. For a workaholic work is so addictive that personal discipline matters little in life. He does not maintain a well-defined

routine, since his scheme of life does not permit such indulgences, as a result he becomes the patient of sleeplessness. Isht Pranam technique of tantropathy and "Baba Shaiya" technique along with following of the model daily routine is more than sufficient for such a person.

One can feel young forever even in advanced age after practising and adopting the technique of tantropathy. Child is supple and agile because of his flexible movement in any direction with ease and comfort. As he grows older, his body gets more rigid and agility level decreases abnormally with it. The ageing process can be delayed by maintaining flexibility of spine, joints and muscles of the body by practising techniques of tantropathy. One can even halt the ageing process by keeping the spinal cord flexible life long. A flexible spine will keep a person agile, young and his nervous system active, ligaments and muscles flexible and elastic as well as blood system improved.

6. Tantropathy has given very much importance to pran-tatva or conscious energy. There is an establishment of conscious energy (Pran) within our body, whose functions, virtues and effects on our mind and body are also narrated in detail in tantrik texts. Now modern scientists are also accepting the establishment and existence of Pran in our body. Pran is called conscious energy in modern science. There are five types of energies according to physical science: (1) light, (2) heat, (3) magnetism, (4) electricity and (5) sound. One type of energy can be converted into another type of energy. "Baba Shaiya" technique converts energies into magnetic energy and

cures the patient from ailments. Life energy is different than the scientific physical energy but it is accepted by them. The electricity-generating centre in the body is called "Reticular activity system". In the depth of the middle of the brain, some brain nerves generate electricity, which spreads inside whole of the brain and generates vibration. The electricity currents operate in different centres of the brain and are connected among themselves. It can be measured by E.E.G. (electro-encephalogram) and it can detect the disease of the head cavity. The flow of conscious energy (Pran) in our body is also accepted by physicians now. For inactiveness and paralysis of muscles of the body, they use E.M.G. (electro-magograph). These are the proofs of the presence of conscious energy in every nerve and muscle. Even in skin a kind of energy is present. And for skin-response system they use galvanic skin response system. When two persons meet, they exchange body energy by touching, embracing or even by seeing. Two people are attracted even when they meet for the first time and sometimes they are distracted. Attraction or distraction is the proof of presence of body electricity. One can push his or her body energy through strong wishes (Shubh Bhawana technique) and magnetic eyes (Jamawant technique) by embracing or by seeing. Even normal touch, hand shake and neck-to-neck touch can exchange human energy to one another vigorously.

Tantra says that Pran is maintaining existence of body by developing, rebuilding, correcting and preserving. Hence Pranmai Kosh, which is enveloped by the 'Annamai Kosh' is alone running and controlling the life. The minutest part of our body is cell, which is electrically charged. Lakhs of genes, which are found in the nucleus of the cell, are known as Patrice (electrically charged) units and in this way modern science has accepted the existence of Pran in each and every minutest part of the body. In every cell negative and positive currents are flowing in and out. It is called depolarisation and repolarisation in scientific language, supporting the description of 'Vyan Vayu' of tantra. Chakra Shodhan - Bhedan technique and Bhuto-Shariro-Mann Shuddhi technique of Tantropathy along with Virasana ruddha simple and Dhwanyatmak Pranayam are sufficient enough to generate life energy for becoming healthy, fit and happy.

7. Toning up the abdominal (Udro Gahwar) muscles will not only give you the flat stomach but will also improve your thorax (Beksho Gahwar) and pelvic cavity (Kati Gahwar) along with your posture and body shape. You will get surprising results in short period if you try to tone the specific muscles of abdomen by practising Maha Mrityunjay technique of tantropathy, which are attached to the upper body at the ribs of thorax cage with the lower body at the pelvis and serve as a bridge between the two, holding the spine erect in its natural position. The mid-section of the body is primarily made up of these two muscle groups. There are not many bones or ligaments in this region, hence it is vital to take care of these muscles.

Four different types of muscles make up the abdominals, starting with the innermost layer called the "transverse abdominis", that runs horizontally surrounding the waist and holds the organs (vital life-running installations) intact. Next is called "Internal obliquus", which runs diagonally starting from the pubic area to the ribs followed by "external obliquus" which runs opposite to the internals. These two groups together help you to twist and turn and to move your waist from side to side. The topmost layer is the "rectum sheath", that runs straight from the pubic region to ribs divided by the "Tinea alba". These muscles help you to bend forward when you want to pick up something from the floor. We may realise the importance after seeing the biology of abdominal cavity, thorax cavity and pelvic cavity for maintaining the fitness, health and happiness, which are already mentioned in thousands year-old tantric texts of India to tone up the muscles and activities of the life-running equipments (organs) situated in these cavities. By the nature (Prakriti), some techniques are developed in tantropathy as Chakra Shodhan-Bhedan technique, Maha Mrityunjaya technique etc.

8. Techniques of tantropathy are designed, shaped and developed in such a way that they work as auto-pressure during our health problems. The ancient Indian art of auto-pressure is believed to be known and practised from 3000 BC onwards for fitness, health and healing. Later this method became more popular in China in the form of outer pressure. Outer pressure method from other person is also popular in India for general health and fitness and still prevalent in rural areas, when there is fever or bodyache. This is purely a tantric method of healing. In such ailment, finger tips of hands are used to rub the hands, legs, chest and back. Actually endocrine glands are connected to all the points on the hands and feet. Each part of the body has a reflection point at the end of these two extremities. So if there is severe pain in

any part of the body, the patient should press the representative points of various organs by stretching the body through the "Angrai technique" of tantropathy. A continuous pressure for even a minute brings relief to the head, joints, muscles, back and abdominal region and helps early recovery. Actually invisible electromagnetic power of the body starts from the tips of the fingers and travels parallel to the body. First it reaches the head and travels backward in a straight line to the toes.

The resistance to the travel of magnetic waves in different directions results in diseases of the body and mind. The best way to overcome the problem of resistance is to press the tips of fingers and to stretch maximum for a few seconds intermittently daily in the morning and evening or perform 'Theiyja Nritya', keeping left hand on the head and right hand on buttock. This gives resistance to diseases. When we press the tips, north-pole wave travels. Thus during the act of compression, a north-pole wave travels and during the act of release a south-pole wave travels in the body. In "Theiyja Nritya", through left hand and hips (which represent south pole) and head and right hand (representing north pole) magnetic waves travel parallel from south to north and north to south poles, removing hindrances that cause ailments. When left hand is kept on head and right hand on the hips with gentle movement along the legs from left to right and right to left for 5 minutes in either sleeping, sitting or walking postures, great relief is felt.

Tantra says that there is no need of outside pressure or massaging, if you are practising Deva mudra and Pashu mudra daily, and that will be sufficient to activate the north pole and south pole of the electro-magnetic power of the body. Practice of the Chakra Shodhan-Bhedan technique of tantropathy, which is a combination of Deva mudra and Pashu mudra, should be practiced for not more than 30 minutes, with empty stomach or after taking one or two glasses of saline lemon water. Foot reflexology is a specialised shoot of the tantric way of auto-pressure, which is developed in the West by Dr Willam Fetzgerald and Eunice Ingham, which is a unique technique. Autopressure by the techniques of tantropathy is the simplest and most effective mode of self-treatment, which is specially effective in the ailments like allergies, asthma, spinal disorders, bronchitis, colds, cramps, ear and eye problems, headache, migraine, gall stones, hay fever, high blood pressure, insomnia, lever conditions, piles etc.

9. Techniques of tantropathy are developed keeping six points of tantra yoga in mind targets: the spine, digestive system, respiratory system, circulatory system, glandular system and nervous system. Tantra declares that if you keep these six functions well, you remain in good health. As a person's age advances, the spinal cord becomes stiff and loses its elasticity. "Isht Pranam" technique of tantropathy helps through bending backwards and forward and twisting sideways on its axis, keeping the spine flexible and nervous system as active as possible. You can improve your digestive system and excretory system by practising these techniques, which flex and contract the abdominal pelvic and thoracic muscles, thereby massaging all the organs of the thorax, abdominal and pelvic cavity and thus activating them.

An efficient digestive system helps the other systems of the body to work at their optimum. A novel technique is of simple echoing (Pratidhwanyatmak Pranayam) technique, which regulates the respiratory and circulatory systems for which neither extra time nor efforts are required. It is only advised to inhale slowly but deeply, filling the lungs to their capacity while sounding 'Om' (Aum) mentally and exhaling slowly with the sound 'M'. The controlled and deep breathing in 'Virasana' has a beneficial effect on the whole respiratory and circulatory systems. There are other benefits too. You have to hold concentration with posture and poses, and this will have sobering effect on the mind and will improve the balance.

Mandukya Upanishad belongs to *Atharva Veda*, which extends god-head (Aum) as the principle of 'Aum'. The guru of Shankaracharya, Guru Gaudepada, says in his 'Vasya': "Masndukyam Ekamevalam a mumkshunam Ekamevalam mumukshunem Vimuktaya." The drop (individual consciousness) merges with the ocean (Supreme consciousness) which leads to liberation mentally and physically (Moksh). 'Aum' consists of three elements: (1) consciousness, (2) body and mind, and (3) supreme consciousness. Our mind consists of past, present and future, involving body and mind, and consciousness has direct link with the supreme consciousness. Repetition of Aum very slowly but mentally, involving respiratory system, daily leads to liberation from its past, present and future ailments (Karma) as well as liberation of soul from sanskara. Gita describes god-head (Om) as the combined light of thousands of suns in the sky. During the practice practitioners are advised to see this light in the triangle above both the eyebrows.

10. Modern living is full of stress and strain and most people want quick relaxation, and for that they use alcohol, smoking, tobacco etc. But these short-cuts do more harm than temporary relief. There are so many short-cut techniques in tantropathy for relaxation which are simple ;but most effective. It helps the mind and body to relax maximum. Simply you have to give the body a chance to unwind, realign, pamper, soothing and re-energise. Give some time to recover and you will perform better, for which you have to include Gyan-Dhyan technique for hand and feet and "Shubh Bhawana" mudra in your daily routine. It works on the pressure points along the meridian channels of energy and for that you need 3 to 5 minutes and all you require is a blanket to sit on the floor. Tantra says that mudras and feelings have innate (complementing, supplementing and implementing) relation. Any feeling whether good or bad will have to produce corresponding poses. Similarly, poses if practiced will certainly produce corresponding feelings.

Gyan-Dhyan mudra techniques

- Sit in Sukhasana (comfortable posture in welcome pose), Abhinandanatmak mudra, folding feet from knee and hand, from elbow, joining palms and touching thorax (Anaahad chakra), opening your palms and fingers of both hands up to wrist by stretching all the fingers to the maximum. Foot sole of legs also touches each other, but open the foot soles up to ankle and stretch all the toes to maximum for a few seconds and relax. Then bend your middle fingers to touch the palms in that position, and try to touch the roots of thumbs and the middle of the thumb and relax.

Dhyan Mudra

☞ Then open the wrist, ankle and knee together by stretching fingers and toes and concentrate on your respiration by watching its coming and going without disturbing it, and count 8 and then relax. Repeat two or three times if you feel so. You can do this even while sitting on the chair or lying on bed, as per your convenience.

☞ Lay on your back, supporting your knees and head on a blanket or carpet or sit in any dhyanasana or sit in a chair with your feet apart. Try to smile slowly. By contracting scalp of your face, eyes and lips, with eyes half open, rest your head, bending slightly forward, and take a few deep breaths and imagine sun is shining down on your triangle above the eyebrows. First you would feel that it is warming the right arm and the whole body as well as you are becoming fresh, alert and relaxed. Repeat it two to three times and then take a good stretch pose (Angrai mudra).

Mann Shuddhi

☞ If you are lying on the bed or sitting on chair, thrash your arms and legs about and have a full-blown tantrum, if possible like toddlers. You will feel more energetic and relaxed. According to tantra, correct stretching of body as a whole in this way dispels lethargy and energises the body and mind both. Angrai mudra is a great stress reducer. Recent scientific researches have proved that tight knotted muscles send uneasy messages to the brain, whereas relaxed muscles send "all well" signals. You should not feel silly while doing this technique. Who cares if it works for your fitness and health.

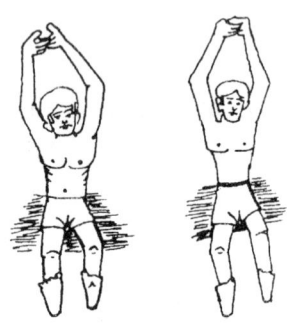

Angrai Mudra

☞ Virasana Ruddh Pranayam is the technique for relieving lower backache. It is one of the simplest and cheapest techniques instantly calming down the body.

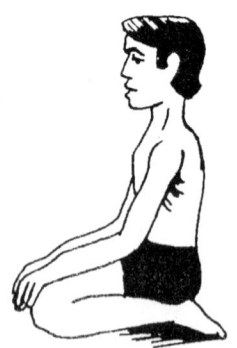

Dhyan Mudra

Sit in Virasana keeping spine straight, giving pressure on hips and inhale slowly and deeply from the bottom of your lungs. Feel your abdomen swell as you inhale, hold for a moment, then relax. Then exhale in your own time. Repeat thrice. The effect is immediate.

Tantra declares that we are all born as sandra (emotionally unstable, uncultured and rustic as animals guided purely by instincts (pleasure principle), but by Sanskara (cultural training, social compulsions and moral obligations) we become a different new person (Sanskaropi Dwijayate). What we think, so we do and as we do, so our mind is. Human sanskar is the conditioning of mind from childhood through repetitions via auto-suggestions, outer suggestions and prestige suggestions. Mostly family members (parents and other relations), society (neighbours, friends, school mates, colleagues etc.) and culture (religion, customs and moral training) influence our moods and behaviour, and what we have learnt is we are today. That is our body clock, as explained by Osteber, a Stockholm doctor. He found in his research that some of us are switched on in the morning and others in the evening. The morning types spring out of bed full of vitality, but during the day they gradually run down. By evening they are only just ticking over, whereas evening types crawl through the morning and do not become fully wound up until supper time.

He says that man is eventually a living clock. Some day you become moody, your partner is emotionally chirpy. He says further that we all are living 24 hour clocks, a part of the larger clock (the universe). The rotating earth represents lines, which in turn forms a part of the rhythmic change of our solar system. He called this daily sequence of our body "circadian rhythm". Scientists have found that we all have traditional obstacles to overcome to sense these rhythms in ourselves and let them guide our life. Bernard Gittlon rightly says, "We are trained to eat when served, not to notice when we are hungry. We are taught to go to lavatory when it is convenient to our teachers, not our bowels. We are directed to do our home-work, when it is convenient for the parents, not our minds." Now more people begin to realise according to the clock inside, which is not natural but conditioned by circumstances, and accordingly each of us every hour of the day is a different person. Chakra Shodhan and Bhedan technique will correct the effect of solar system. Certainly Tantra says that every action of human being from visiting lavatory to eating and sleeping is worship. You have to do that timely within the framework of devotion expectation and surrender. Actually nothing is static in this universe. Nothing to worry. Every thing is changing either by nature or by practice. Condition your mind by practising the techniques of tantropathy and following a model daily routine regularly.

- The technique of tantropathy is the method of tapping energy. Our body receives internal and external energies from the five basic elements that compose the universe. Internal energy is received in the form of food we eat (earth), the fluid we take (water) and the air we breathe (sky). We receive external energy in the from of heat and light (fire) as well as vibrations and sound (space). When the internal and external energies are balanced, our mental and physical conditions are harmonious. If the intake of one or more elements is not in proportion to the constitution of the person, one experiences disharmony, leading to a gamut of physical, emotional and mental afflictions. With ill-health and lack of peace of mind, one's level of vibration also lowers and there is tremendous dissipation of energies, leading to problems at work, losses in business, inviting disputes, anxiety at home and difficulty in relation.

The science of energy cycle aims at aligning the energy cycle with the magnetic axis of the earth, enabling it to attract all the positive energies of the universe. To activate the energy cycle, Dhyanasana, Vajrasana and Yantrasana are used in tantra. 'Om' mantra is practiced in Vajrasana. Isht Pranam mudra is practiced in Vajranasana and different tantric yantras are used in Yantrasana at the time of puja. Yantrasana affects our body's gravitational centre, human navel. Above all asanas should be practiced along with yantra and mantra as per the meditation technique of tantropathy for taking full benefit out of it in the morning, preferably between 5 and 6 a.m. Every cycle is a pragmatic method to achieve equilibrium between internal and external energies in order to attain healthy body and mind.

☞ We can even help enhance concentration and memory or defuse stress through the practice of the techniques of tantropathy along with taking the food prescribed. These are mostly seasonal fruits and vegetables, which are specially offered to lord Shiva-Parvati in worshipping. The right food can also help enhance concentration and memory or defuse stress to some extent undoubtedly. Hard nuts and brightly coloured fruits are generally treated as brain food. Ber (plum), bael, nariyal (coconut), guava, jamun and other Indian fruits have been scientifically proved to be loaded with vitamins, minerals and phyto-chemicals that maintain brain health. By taking these fruits mood, motivation and mental performance are greatly influenced. Though you may be unaware of this but people could take it as an indicator of the way you will react to events in your life.

Recent research shows that our every thought and feeling is using neuro-chemicals or neurotransmitter (acetylcholine), which is essential for memory formation, maintenance and establishing the lines of communication between brain cells. Serotonin is another famous neurotransmitter, which is involved in sleep, sensory perception, temperature regulation, control of mood and anxiety reduction. Apart from these, Dopamine-Epinephrine and Neuro-penephrine are collectively called catecholamines, which control aroused anxiety state. All these neurotransmitters are made available to the brain from amino-acids and other substances present in the food, and through proper exercise. Amino-acid tryptophan is found in protein rich food like wheat, rice, pulse, fish, and meat. Acetylcholine is made from the fat-like vitamin

"B" complex, which is found in fruits, leafy vegetables, egg, yolks etc. Improper dietary patterns, diseases and ageing deplete the neurotransmitters and in such cases choline-loaded food should be taken. Dietary fats that are broken down into fatty acids go into hormones, which are critical to body metabolism. These fats constitute the outer membrane of every cell in the body, including those in the brain. Among fatty acids, notemic acid (N-3) and notamic acid (N-6) are essential and they have to be obtained from vegetarian diet. Walnut oil and fish oil are rich in these acids. Apart from these, regular practice of "Pitri yagya" technique, concentrating on light with proper poses and meditation, you will possess good memory, intelligence and strength. "Om" mantra should be recited melodiously aligning with respiration, and its continuity and unity should be maintained in Virasana at least for a few minutes after taking meal. This posture and technique will take care of your gravitational point of the body properly.

- The attitude toward life has total impact on our health, fitness and happiness. There is a close relation between illness and nurturing negative thoughts. To become rigid, rough, unyielding and totally negative is our attitude towards life. You might be a victim of circumstances and feel that life has nothing good to offer you any more. But this attitude toward your life is not going to give you benefit nor get you anywhere, rather would give very definite signals to people around you. Though you may be unaware of this, people could take it as an indication of the way you will react to events in your life.

Our personality is often influenced by incidents that take place in the early years of our life. These events can change the directional forces, which bring an occasional change into our lives and our mood patterns considerably. Then often the harshness of life can leave you bitter and very negative attitude towards things that can come into contact with us. The tendency to criticise others and put people down is the negative part of our life. Our personality esteem is nothing but what colours our attitude towards others. Our life patterns are written by the time we are 5 years old. If one's childhood had been negative, then one grows up to be negative person. One does not have to develop the techniques of fighting all that to become a person with a positive outlook. "Karma gyan udbodhan vidhi" is such a technique of tantropathy. Parents should be cautious and careful towards their gestures, nuances and subtle messages before kids. We should not forget that children learn what you put into practice, not learn what you tell them. We should always try to re-inforce positive attitude in our kids. All we have certain desires as "to be loved", "to be appreciated" and "to be recognised." If these remain unfulfilled, negative feelings start accumulating. Rejection will destroy the self-esteem, whereas acceptance will build it. Start your day at 5 to 5.30 a.m. with a model daily routine technique or time budget technique of tantropathy. Believe firmly that this helps you to feel alive and energetic throughout the day, and you must practice "Isht

Pranam" technique regularly at least for 4 weeks for 20 to 30 minutes daily.

- The life span can be extended by practising the techniques of tantropathy regularly, which also makes the life easier. These techniques are stepping stones to make your time stretch and life comfortable. If you are too lazy to change your bad habits and faulty life style, the good news for you is that there are a few tantropathic tricks for you. Here are some of the weird, wonderful and scientifically proven theories on things that add years to your life. Shubh Bhawana and Prayer techniques are certainly life strengthening. Tantric texts including *Durga Saptashati* are full of such prayer techniques. Shubh Bhawana technique is being given in this book in detail. These techniques should be repeated twice a day in the morning before leaving the bed and in the evening after going to bed. After sitting in Virasana for a minute only you will see a magic effect within 4 weeks after the practice.

National Institute of Health Research in America claims that praying for long life could work miracles. A research report conducted by the Institute reveals that church goers have a lower mortality rate. No doubt, comfort, hope and social support help in lowering the mortality. But Danial Weeks, a clinical psychologist at the Royal Edinburgh Hospital, believes "it is spirituality that counts". He further states, "any form of faith, be it mysticism or even witchcraft is life strengthening." Tantra declares, "Prani Paten Pariprashnan Sewaya", which means surrender completely before Isht or the larger aims and objects

(Pranipaten). We are connected with the society physically, mentaly and spiritually. Therefore, we should be well equipped with all the ways and means of the development of society along with our development and to search out the solution of all its problems (Pariprashnan), and 'Sewaya' means to serve the society selflessly as a responsible member. The true spirit of 'Sewaya' is that if you want good for yourself, do good to others. My observation is that practice of Shubh Bhawana and Isht Pranam techniques with any from of faith and belief is certainly life strengthening.

There are effective cathartic elements in every culture of the word, such as prayer before the deity in Hindu culture, confession before father in christian culture, etc. Group kirtan, group dance, singing bhajan are also cathartic. Auto prestige and mass suggestion techniques of tantropathy are based on this cultural heritage and it is very much effective for psychological, emotional and spiritual healing; Shubh Bhawana technique is one of them.

- A newcomer to these techniques and tantropathic methods usually gives up early or seeks only the initial benefits and gains on specific results. But a little persistence leads to a sense of well being, which opens a whole new world. The author of this book and discoverer of tantropathic techniques for health, fitness and happiness is a regular practitioner of these techniques, who has benefited through a profound impact of outlook, confidence and overall feeling of satisfaction. Soon you may realise that practice of these techniques is more than a fitness activity. It will help you bring back your childhood, enthusiasm and activity as well as youthfulness. As your body tones up, so will your overall being: you will feel good about yourself and the people around you.

Always remember four Guru Mantras — drink liquids profusely, exercise regularly, smile profusely and control your mind through positive attitude. You will feel high. Self-esteem is the best recipe for good looks and courage. Stretching the frontiers of mind (forehead) is the best path to a healthy attitude and feeling good. Tantropathy revives, develops and reshapes the techniques of age-old traditional (Tantra-yoga) consciousness. It helps make people aware of the necessity of being healthy, fit and happy and to have a beautiful, healthy, magnetic and pleasing personality. In the last few years here has been a gradual change in the mental set up of the people around the world in general and Indian people in particular towards holistic treatment, especially Tantra-yoga therapy.

Today western people and especially youngsters are fed up with the allopathic medicines and sophisticated equipments of fitness. Awareness of health and fitness is a global phenomenon. In India western culture is popular; hence naturally this trend of awareness is also prevalent here. To put it bluntly, were are aping the west, but for a good cause. In tantropathy chilled shower for health is derived from Kartik Snan of Indian culture. Auto massaging or self-massaging for different shuddhis (cleansing), Shodhan

TANTROPATHY

Bhedan Kriya mentioned in tantrik text, jacuggi from Shiva's Tandav Nritya and Theiya Nritya and technique of surrendering to Supreme consciousness from different Abhinandanatmak Pranam are used specially for slimming, skin care and de-stressing treatment. The technology we use for fat loss is based purely on tantra-yoga.

☞ The aim of the techniques of tantropathy is to increase the energy, vigour and vitality by stimulating the various channels of our body, thereby keeping the vital organs in good and healthy state. There are two types of major energies in our body, the one with which we are born and whose constant flow is maintained by proper eating, ample drinking, deep breathing and daily exercising. It is preserved through practising in moderation. Building and generation of these energies is in our hand by practising the techniques of tantropathy to maintain health and vitality by doing away with any blockage or depletion. This energy flows in the body through meridian channels (chakras). Every meridian is associated with an organ, and when it is pressed by poses and postures along the length of a channel that passes through a problematic area, the flow of energy is stimulated. This helps the organ without touching it.

☞ The special technique of tantropathy for getting on is Ujabuk mudra (Hang loose technique). Hanging loosely and getting on mentally are the special features of this technique. We know that if you are all hyped up, you are less likely to succeed in what you are doing. A famous psychologist William James once said, "It is a relaxed and easy worker who works most efficiently. Tension and anxiety mixed all at once in the mind are the surest drags to steady progress and hindrances to success." If one has to succeed in life, relaxation is essential. It is a simple case of demand and supply. Work requires energy and there is limited amount of energy. When one is taut and rigid and this activity uses extra energy, hence obviously the amount of energy available for work is reduced.

Emotions and tension are closely related, and in this condition we never wholly give ourselves up in the work place or at the home. We breathe 18 or 19 times instead of 16 times a minute and never quite breathe out. In such a tense state of mind and body, keep your legs, hands and body muscles half contracted, open your eyelids, contracting the upper eyelid up and lower eyelid down to the maximum and look wildly. Hold this position for a few seconds, then move your eyeballs right to left and left to right and then up to down and down to up eight times, then relax, watch your breathing without disturbing it for a minute only and you will be normal. In this state alone you can be productive. This is Jamawant mudra.

In a situation where we tend to grow nervous, anxious and overburdened, we should deliberately keep our nerves unstrained. Fearful, anxious and forbidding mental attitudes can be reduced through the practice of the Ujabuk technique of tantropathy and can be prevented altogether.

Procedure of Ujabuk technique: Hang loosely during sleeping, standing, walking and sitting, keeping mentally and physically free of tension. Whether sleeping, standing, walking, talking or sitting, give pressure on hips, keep spine erect, and keep the muscles of hand and feet loose. See your breathing is coming in and going out, from the bottom of abdomen, maintaining the scalp of your face stretched. Every moment keep in good mood, free from tension and anxiety. Many people get tightened up while waiting for a bus or train or before a business interview. They force themselves into a state bordering on muscular spasm. Even while listening concerts or delivering lectures, people seem to be listening or speaking with their bodies rather than through their ears and minds.

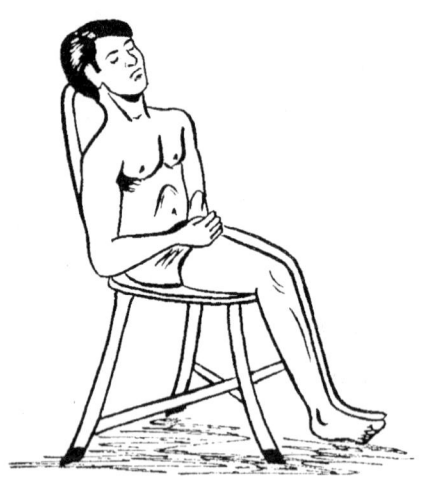

Ujabuk technique

TANTROPATHY

Such speakers and writers develop speaker cramps or writer cramps through unnecessary muscular contractions. You have seen sages and speakers frequently tightening up their neck and throat muscles especially on high notes and emotional passages. This is detrimental not only to their specific organs but also dangerous to their general health.

By tauting the whole body we spend useless energy. Save your energy by practising Ujabuk mudra and Isht Pranam technique, sleep in Baba Shaiya technique, and be healthy and fit. If you are feeling very much tensed, close your eyes slowly and lightly, let your jaw and hand loose, suspend your tongue and breathe deeply from the bottom of abdomen. You will be as good as new. Our sincere advice is that without thinking of the outcome or dwelling on the wisdom, act fearlessly, thinking before action is good because we have no control on both. Success and failure as well as worries and anxiety would not change things. Work to live and live to work. Workaholics invite many dangerous ailments and cut their life short. Techniques of tantropathy are more for improving your postures than vigorous exercise which you need for your longevity, pleasure and success. They act on both body and mind, and also improve the spiritual sense of behaviour simultaneously.

☞ Nirmimekh Varjan technique of tantropathy (better than hypnosis) is an accepted way of giving up bad habits like smoking, chewing tobacco or drinking alcohol. It can also save the physical, psychological and spiritual problems. Even asthma, eczema, irritable bowel syndrome and high blood pressure can be cured by using this technique. It is discussed separately in the last chapter of this book.

☞ *Cathartic technique of tantropathy:* There are effective cathartic elements in every culture of the world. Prayer before deity in Hindu culture and confessions before father in christian culture are some of them. Group kirtan and bhajan are also kind of cathartic. Auto prestige and mass suggestion techniques of tantropathy as well as Shubh Bhawana technique are based on these cultures and heritages, and these are very much effective in psychological, emotional and spiritual healing. It will be discussed elaborately elsewhere.

☞ Endocrine glands of our body control our growth. These glands are (a) thyroid glands, (b) pituitary glands, (c) thymus glands and (d) some sexual glands. The pituitary gland controls the growth of bones. When a child is born his thymus gland is very large; but it starts shrinking after the age of 13 to 14 years. At that stage sex glands start controlling the growth of the body. The body attains full maturity at the age of 20-22 years and after that the growth stops. The gland responsible for physical growth becomes less active after this age and we start ageing. But in tantropathy growing up does not matter. What matters is climbing up, keeping stress at bay, having sound sleep following model daily routine and getting into shape.

☞ Techniques of tantropathy are also used as medical therapy to overcome our physical limitations. Our mind and Sukhshm Sharir (ethereal body) are used for medical therapy in tantropathy. You can call it psychospirituo-technology, in which human consciousness and electronic medium merge. We can communicate with all the body's cells ordering them to shape up like in Chakra Shodhan-Bhedan technique, which may be called mini telepathic communication. Actually we and all creatures of the universe are connected mentally. This is the reason that the birds and animals respond to our love and affection. Mind to mind replaces computer to computer in tantropathy as the quickest and most preferred method of transmitting power, to get fit, healthy and happy. Nirmimekh Varjan technique is one of them. It is based on prominent declaration that each individual consciousness is the integral part of Supreme consciousness and rapport can be established through the practice of this technique.

☞ *Adhyatmik (religious) techniques of tantropathy:* All the techniques of tantropathy have Adhyatmic essence of Indian origin. Mental wavering in general and physical activity in particular are seen Lila (funny play). All the miraculous mental and physical activities of Lord Krishna are called Krishna lila for this reason. Spirituality is socialising. Kids resist as soon as they suspect that sports are being pushed on them as something that is good for parents only, not for them.

Physical activity seems painless to kids or adults when it is not a part of daily life. You might have observed that many kids never saw their parents walking to a destination or using the stairs when there is lift available. They inherit this habit and develop apathy towards physical activity. Without following model daily routine given in this book, one cannot develop interest in technique of tantropathy and will not be benefited much. Hence it is essential for the practitioners to follow model daily routine and practice in group.

::::::::

CHAPTER 3

- Sleeplessness vs sound sleeping 116
- Stress reaction vs relaxation response 128
- General fatigue vs life style 143
- Cure constipation, heart burn and headache through toning up of abdominal and rectal muscles 152
- Headache 161
- Control of diabetes and impotency through tantropathy..166
- Chandrayan technique for obesity 171

SLEEPLESSNESS VS SOUND SLEEPING

It is said that sleep is measured by its depth, not by its length. If a person is deprived of his sleep long enough, he will become insane. It is true that lack of sleep severely affects all mental processes. The brain works through the night, doing some house-keeping of its own. Nerve networks that have remained unused during the day are activated and exercised. Some developing and maturing of brain circuits also take place during certain phases of sleep. Researchers believe that facts collected during the day are sorted out and consolidated in memory during sleep. So the popular belief that "Sleeping over a problem" helps you see things closely in sound sleep may be a scientific fact. The tantrics knew the role of sleeping posture (Shaiya) for sound sleeping and considered that "Tathagat Shaiya', in which Lord Buddha was sleeping, is the perfect. Different tantric schools of Hindus also follow their own observations and findings on sleep.

Role of sleep in getting good health, fitness and happiness

Sleep is one of he most important activities in our life. When the body and mind are tired, sleep induces rest and helps it recuperate. Sleep is just like our nourishing food. It is essential for our physical, mental and spiritual health. Every body needs certain amount of sound sleep everyday depending upon one's physical, mental and spiritual condition. Actually we are living in the age of excessive competition, pollution, adulteration and economic domination, and we are harvesting tension, anxiety and sleeplessness in such a stressed and strained situation, which does not allow the brain to switch off during the night. Due to sleeplessness (insomnia), the person becomes irritable. He may have a heavy head or frequent headaches, may become tired or disinterested in normal activities and can even suffer from constipation or catch cold. At this stage many people run after tranquilisers and sleeping pills and often become addicted to these drugs.

Sleeplessness is the outcome of modern civilization and style of life. Tantropathy (Tanra-yoga therapy) has discovered and developed "Baba Shaiya", a technique to calm tension and anxiety, to slow down the mind easily and effectively. It is a definite posture and pose of sound sleeping. Isht Pranam is another technique based on tantric practices like swagat, sannidhya and sashtang pranam (welcome, nearness and surrender postures and poses). If a person practices 'Isht Pranam' in the morning after finishing morning duties for 30 minutes and in evening before going to bed and sleep in 'Baba Shaiya' everyday at least for 4 weeks, even problems like insomnia can be eliminated.

We sleep more soundly in darkness than in light

Sound sleeping is deep sleeping. It can change our life entirely. We relax fully after sound sleeping. Actually our health, fitness and happiness depend on postures and poses at the time of sleep, which keep our spine straight, giving soothing, relaxing and pleasant feeling at the time of sleeping in darkness. This will itself create favourable and comfortable background for sound sleeping. We sleep soundly in darkness than in light, because our behaviour is controlled by chemical transmitter system of brain.

Serotonin-secreting neurons of our brain spread out their fibres to suppress the activity of reticula and brain in darkness. Thus the system promotes sleep. Dark blue night bulb of zero watt helps the system by giving soothing effect in brain. Neurons secrete serotonin profusely. The melatonin-secreting neurons of our brain spread out their fibres in light to arouse reaction. Hence never try to sleep in light. We should not take our sleep lightly. "As we think, so we are". Hence do not retire in bed without welcoming the sleep in anticipation. Repeat the following sentences thrice mentally, "I salute and welcome, sleep. Please come immediately so that I will sleep soundly". Here expectation of sleep counts.

Process of cooling down to sleep

You know it very well that after closing eyes you are not feeling asleep. Sleeping is not a thing that will come first after closing eyes. In fact sleep is a complex system of winding down. Several factors fall into place before the body can shut its shop for the night. Body temperature is one such factor, which must come down to a certain extent before the body can enter the sleep phase. The body mechanism for sleep becomes inefficient as one grows older and the body does not cool down automatically. This is one of the reasons of the old people for not falling to sleep so quickly. To beat this problem, sleep experts suggest that about 3 to 5 hours before bed time one should 'heat up' a bit by brisk walking or working even in kitchen garden. This will create sufficient difference between their peak day time warmth and bed time temperature.

A study, involving 50 to 5 years old people, reveals that early evening, just 1½ hours before taking meal,

TANTROPATHY

'Isht Pranam' for 20 minutes along with 'Tandava Nritya' for 3 minutes and sleep through 'Baba Shaiya' brought down the time taken to fall asleep soundly from 25 to 30 minutes to 5 to 10 minutes and they stayed in sleep an hour longer than before. It will be better of try formation of hobby technique, 'Bhuta Yoga', by taming animals or birds or planting trees and keeping flower pots. Tryptophan is an amino acid needed to make serotonin, a chemical in the brain that helps induce sleep. Milk is naturally rich in tryptophan. There is a popular ritual to take a glass of warm milk slightly sweetened before going to bed. For good sleeping take vitamins and minerals from vegetables and fruits and avid or reduce consumption of stimulants like alcohol, quit smoking as well as heavy and large meals.

'Siesta' to boost your life span

Scientists say a daily "power nap" can boost your life span as well as your performance. Greek study found that men who took daily "siestas" suffered fewer heart problems. Research in Britain shows that people with chronic sleep problem have a higher mortality rate than those sleeping at least 6½ to 8 hours. "Drowsiness is an urgent warning and that should not be ignored particularly in situations where dozing, inattention or impaired performance could lead to catastrophe", said Dr William Dement, Director, Sleep Disorders Clinic of U.S.A. A good night sleep contributes as follows:

- Without adequate rest, the immune system has difficulty in defending against disease-causing microorganisms. Surveys in America show that compared with normal sleepers, chronic, insomniacs develop more illness and recover from them more slowly.

☞ People with illness should be sent straight of bed, because increased need for sleep is the body's way of orchestrating recovery. Most growth and recovery from illness occur during sleep, specifically during the deepest or delta stage.

☞ Sound sleeping at least for 7 hours and more increases longevity, whereas people who sleep for 6 hours or less have greater mortality. A 9 years study by the California Department of Health showed this.

Proper sleeping and relaxing postures and poses can change the life entirely

The age-old tantra teaches that your health, fitness and happiness depend on proper postures and poses that keep your spine straight, and exert pressure on hips; while walking, standing, sitting and sleeping give you relaxing, soothing and pleasant feeling. 'Baba Shaiya' is a sleeping posture and pose discovered and developed on the basis of tantric texts of Buddhism, Jainism and Hinduism. Buddhists were great tantrics and they researched, discovered and developed many tantric ways of health, fitness and happiness along with spiritual salvation. But with the downfall of India, we have lost a great treasure and what is available is not impossible but a bit difficult to find out something from its vast remaining treasure.

TANTROPATHY

Salient features of 'Baba Shaiya':

☞ To lie down in bed on back and sleep is called Demon posture of sleeping (Pret Shaiya), in which you have fearful dreams and there will be bad sound from both the nostrils because of undue pressure of thorax on lungs and heart. This posture is also not good for sound sleeping.

Pret Shaiya

☞ We have magnetic power in our body's upper part from navel (gravitational centre of the body) which is positive pole, and lower part from navel

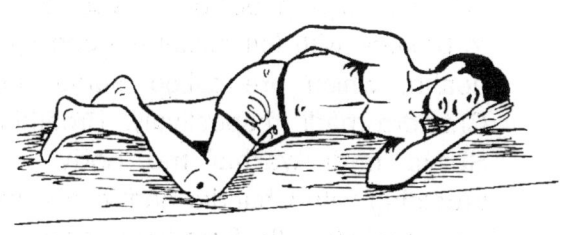

Shakti Shaiya (Kamottejak Shaiya)

which is negative pole. Similarly, left hand of the body is negative and right hand is positive pole. This position may vary from person to person. In 'Baba Shaiya' magnetic circuit of the body is connected and completed by keeping right hand on back and left hand on the middle of the forehead as well as right leg on the knee of left leg and vice-versa.

☞ There is a Guru Chakra in the middle of the forehead and just parallel to the triangle (trikuti). This chakra is most sensitive and has hypnotic powers. If you concentrate even for a few minutes, you will be self-hypnotised. In 'Baba Shaiya', Guru chakra is stimulated by touching it with the first phalange of the thumb and concentrating on it. "Shavasana" along with "Abhinandanatmak mudra" and comfortable bed with a pillow one has to go to bed after sitting in Virasana (Hero posture) for 5 to 10 minutes to stimulate the body's gravitation centre (navel).

(i) We breathe either with both nostrils or in turn from left to right and from right to left automatically. Tantra says that to breathe with right nostril is good for physical aspect and to breathe with left nostril is good for mental health, which are called Surya nadi and Chandra nadi respectively. Breathing with Surya nadi warms the body, whereas breathing with Chandra nadi cools physically and mentaly both. Breathing position can be altered from left to right nostril and from right to left nostril.

(ii) 'Baba Shaiya' is a posture of sleeping comfortably and relaxed, lying on right side in lion posture of sleep (Simha Shaiya), so you can breathe with left nostril during the sleep. This is the proper posture of sound sleeping.

(iii) Sex-stimulating sleeping posture (Kamottejak Shaiya) is to sleep while lying on left side, in which you breathe through right nostril, which is not good for sound sleeping. Avoid this sleeping posture as much as you can. For sciatica patient if one goes to one specialist, he may put you to bed rest for 4 weeks and not even allow to visit the toilet. But if the same patient with exactly the same symptoms goes to another specialist, he may be advised immediately to undergo a course of strenuous physiotherapy exercises. I have personally treated some such patients with the techniques of tantropathy. I feel that if the specialists can decide between two diametrically opposite therapies, it seems reasonable to place the burden of selection on a tantropath, who will correctly advise certain poses and postures in place of complete bed rest or strenuous exercises.

When a man weighing 70 kg stands erect, the pressure within his lumbar discs rises to approximately 142 kg. But when he lies down in bed, pressure immediately drops, to roughly 20 kg, and in sound sleeping the pressure remains minimal or nominal. This reduction in intra-disc pressure can be beneficial, when pain is being caused by the pressure of a bulging disc on a spine nerve. Bed rest with sound sleeping for at least 8 to 10 hours also relaxes the postural muscles of the back and pelvis. But total bed rest carries some risks.

Procedure

Lie down on back in bed and slowly turn left side from the leg and then right side, stretching your body five times. Then consolidate your position in right side, keeping palm on the pillow touching the middle of your forehead, parallel to triangle (trikuti) with first phalange of thumb. Stretch your right leg and lay the left ankle to right knee slowly, touching the bed with right knee. Adjust yourself in this posture comfortably with welcome pose, thinking 'you will have sound sleep'.

Baba Shaiya

Rest without sound sleeping and mobility is no rest

Today rest is a universal panacea. The overworked businessman, on the verge of nervous breakdown, takes long vacation from his job. The patient recovering from a major operation is sent away to a nursing home to convalesce. Undoubtedly rest and time are the great healers but, like other powerful remedies, they are also not without their untoward side-effects. Rest with sound sleep for 8 hours is sufficient, but after that mobility is essential.

Complete bed rest may be seen as the sanest and safest option for recent back or other injuries or ailments, but no two specialists would agree on when or how it should be applied.

- In the first place enforced idleness leads to rapid muscle wasting, which makes the back weaker and more prone to subsequent strain.
- It also hampers the circulation, which slows down the healing of damaged tissues.
- It retards the damaged area of congestion.

Rest means the relaxing state of body and mind both at night in sound sleeping for 7 to 8 hours and lowered mobility of muscles and joints of the body along with positive attitude and feeling in mind with a 2 hours nap at noon. Rest is a physical, mental and spiritual process. Mobility of muscles is a physical process and sound sleeping is the mental process, whereas positive attitude and pleasant feeling are the ingredients of spiritual relaxation. In the absence of these processes rest cannot be imagined. Equally important, mobility favours the formation of restrictive scar tissues whenever a muscle, joint or ligament is injured or there is other ailment, when there is an immediate flow of blood to the damaged issues. This leads to the formation of blood clot, which contains a mass of protein fibres (called fibrin) together with thousands of fibroblasts, the cells responsible for the formation of new fibrous tissues. Within 24 hours of initial injury, a dense network of fibrous tissues is laid down to repair the wounds in a pattern, that is totally dependent on the mechanical forces prevailing at the time. The damaged ligaments or muscles are gently used as they heal through 'Mrit Sanjiwani' technique of tantropathy (discovered and developed after 20 years of experimentation by the author) which uses body channel through ethereal cleanliness of body (Sharir Shuddhi), ethereal cleanliness of mind (Mann Shuddhi) and ethereal cleanliness (Bhut Shuddhi). It includes posture, poses, mantra and yantra properly, rhythmically and systematically. In this process Dharna and Dhyan come automatically with continuity, unity and regularity after practising 20 minutes daily in the morning. It acts as a natural tranquillizer. Researchers at the Mind Body Institute (India), found that it quietens the nervous system, causing a measurable drop in blood pressure and heart rate. The breathing deepens, muscles relax and even capillaries are strengthened. The brain activity changes as well. The number of rapid waves goes down, whereas the serene alpha and delta waves increase. An experienced practitioner of this technique can even drop at that state, while he is still awake.

Sleeplessness phobia

The question arises; 'are you really sleepless. Once a journal *World Medicine* conducted a survey to find out the solution of this question. The topper was, "Doc, I can't sleep well". But tests done in laboratories show that "Sleepless" folk get more sleep than they believe. It is the anxiety and loneliness of wakeful moments that leaves them worn out in the morning. The body usually takes as much sleep as it needs. An adult sleep requirement may be as low as 5 hours a night. If such a person lies next to a person who snores through 10 hours a night, he is sure to develop insomnia. If you can get through your day without drowsiness, stop worrying about insomnia and start thinking about how to spend the extra hours available to you. Lying around in bed, if you are not able to sleep, will affect the quality of slumber. Sleep is like a liquid, if you spread it over a large area, the amount and quality of sleep would decrease. If you have difficulty in falling asleep, you are probably going to bed with the day's irritations, agitations and worries still buzzing in your mind. Experts suggest a "winding down time" before getting into bed by practising the techniques of tantropathy. Spend 5 minutes in Virasana and sleep in "Baba Shaiya". Even good sleeper should not be surprised if leaving tea or certain medication suddenly start affecting your sleep.

::::::::

STRESS REACTION VS RELAXATION RESPONSE

Stress reaction

People who are living next to busy road or working in factory, may learn to live with the noise, though after formation of habit, they may eventually stop noticing that. But that does not mean that the noise pollution has stopped affecting their physical and mental health. These effects are not exactly life threatening but they do add up over time. Actually people coming from noisy work places are more irritable, aggressive and exhausted, as shown by recent studies. Working at high decibel work places like airport or heavy industries raises the possibility of stress-related ailments, such as heart disease, peptic ulcers, hypertension and migraine, which are noise sensitive. It drains mental energy, efficiency and productivity.

In the contemporary corporate world, man-machine is a classic proverb. A person goes to sleep at odd hours and often does not sleep at all for a few hours. He works 12 to 14 hours a day without a conventional weekly holiday. He manages anyhow a breakfast before rushing to the office and his lunch is a hasty exercise just in case he is in a position to spare some thought for food in the busy afternoon. At night it is dinner time but he can eat it very little, since his mind is focused on the file or problems he has left unchecked at office or working place. He broods a lot, eats little, works like a maniac and would love working more. He can be called modern day workaholic, a man for whom work is so addictive that personal discipline matters little in life.

TANTROPATHY

The workaholic does not maintain a well defined routine, since his scheme of life does not permit any such indulgence. He is rarely on time for proper lunch and dinner, eats a lot of junk food and his nutrition level grows alarmingly low. The workaholic develops signs of internal weakness, whereas his physical stress remains unmitigated; on top of this he catches up on his sleep while he can. Due to excessive work there can be hypertension, which can have an adverse impact, leading to heart attack or sometimes enlargement of the heart. The latter is equally lethal and can lead to heart failure. Such a situation can even lead to various problems, like nervous breakdown, insomnia, acidity or ulcer. Such a situation can aggravate the condition of the diabetic and asthma patients. For workaholic stress is a serious problem and can lead to an increase in blood pressure. Blood pressure or no blood pressure, workaholic goes on.

Stress also causes alopecia. It is characterised by patches of hairlessness where the skin underneath looks normal. There is evidence to suggest that it may be stress related as well as it could be linked to a poor diet. Medical treatment such as surgery and certain drugs, including the pill, steroids and cancer drugs can also trigger it. Workaholic should try to make sure that he manages to get adequate sleep. In other words, he should be able to sleep at least for 6½ hours and also try to have short nap of about 45 minutes in the afternoon. 'Baba Shaiya' is also a stress-relieving exercise and immensely helpful for those who need to carry on till late in the night without pause. Corporate houses should realise the importance of stress management, and should once a while organise special programmes inviting tantropath experts to demonstrate techniques for managing stress. Another technique is "Isht Pranam", the key to spiritual bliss and stress management, and for which only 20 to 25 minutes will be required every day in the morning.

Formation of hobby technique of tantropathy (Bhut Yagya technique) is equally important for stress management. Stress seems to be big bad guy of the day, which is something to be avoided at all cost. But we should not forget that, like bad guys, it has positive side as well. Moderate casual stress is necessary and inevitable for the progress in life, because it alerts you to potentially bad situations and gears you up to meet physical and mental challenges. Stress sharpens our senses and helps us focus on the task at hand. The heart pumps faster, so that more blood goes to our brain and limbs, and muscles become tight and ready to go into action. Stress is our ally, when we have to act quickly in an emergency. It is only when stress is too high in challenging situations and too frequent that is damaging. Not only bad events but any thing that needs emotional re-adjustment is stress making. Getting married, starting a new job or business or facing personal, social or financial problems are stressful events. Only dead person can be freed from stress. Hence stress is a common phenomenon. What we have to do is to manage efficiently and effectively for healthy, successful, magnetic and pleasant personality.

Relaxation response

It is a well-known fact that an overactive, disturbed mind can trigger off a stress reaction in the body, raising blood pressure, pounding heart and tense muscles. Powerful negative thoughts can also leave a person drained of physical energy. Fortunately our mind is expressed through our eyes first and then vocal cord (throat) and muscles. Tantra says, "A stress and strain of mind can be cooled, calmed and relaxed through the channels of man-body connection as and when required." The mind-body connection can also be used to switch off the stress response and calm a tense and agitated mind through the techniques of tantropathy. The difference is, the stress response kicks instantly and un-invited but the relaxation response needs the focused effort through Dharna technique of tantropathy (Chakra Shodhan-Bhedan Vidhi) and "Isht Pranam". Dharna technique includes ethereal cleanliness of universal body (Bhut Shuddhi), ethereal cleanliness of physical body (Sharir Shuddhi) and ethereal cleanliness of mind (Mann Shuddhi).

'Isht Pranam' includes Abhinandanatmak mudra (welcome pose), Ardh Pranam (Nearness pose) and Sashtang Pranam (Surrender pose), traditionally and systemically focusing Bij Mudra and Guru Mantra rhythmically, unitedly and continuously. Regular practice of these techniques of tantropathy acts as natural tranquilizer. In a stress reaction our mind wanders like kite without thread in sky and we forget the natural art of bringing it back. In relaxation response we recall the natural art of calming and cooling down the mind. When we are in close contact with any thing man or machinery, regularly we learn its nature automatically and also develop its love. Practising of Dharna technique and 'Isht Pranam' regularly maintains close contact of man and machinery to develop love and to know its nature closely by utilizing mind-body connection. It quietens the nervous system, causing a measurable drop in blood pressure and heart rate. The breathing deepens and muscles relax as well as the brain activity changes. The number of rapid waves goes down unexpectedly. A study of African - American hypertensive persons revealed that the practice of mind-body involvement for 20 minutes daily in the morning and evening brought down the blood pressure by an average of 11 points in the upper number and six points in lower number. The results were only half as good in people who were simply told to relax.

Beware of stress

Stress that affects many bodily processes can aggravate the damage caused by free radicals. But short-lived stress may not cause much damage at the cellular level. Free radicals are chemical molecules with a missing electron. In the absence of partner, an electron turns very reactive and unstable. It will seek out another electron for pairing and returning to a stable state and then cause further damage to the other existing normal cells. Actually free radicals are formed daily within through normal body processes. Either these toxins should be eliminated by our body regularly or we have to fight diseases. Air pollution, radiation (exposure to sunlight), insecticides and herbicides encourage the formation of free radicals. These free radicals are highly unstable and reactive, having enough potential of causing severe damage to the cell structure. They have potential to induce cancer, heart diseases, inflammation, arthritis of joints, brain degeneration and acceleration of the ageing process, and can damage the brain cells.

Antioxidants (free radical compounds that can give up

one of their electrons without turning destructive themselves) can neutralise and normalise these free radicals, thereby stopping their terrorist activities, Antioxidants, which are also chemically designed to diffuse the destructive free radicals, are abundant in green and leafy vegetables, fresh seasonal fruits, positive attitude and exercise, along with following regular daily routine. In fact you can give your cells a powerful and youthful portion by feeding them antioxidants and regularly following the routine along with exercises. When a person is irritated and agitated or depressed or anxious, it is normally blamed on stressful events or his natural temperament. But recent research has unearthed another possible explanation for negative moods: mineral deficiency. They discovered that moods, emotions and behaviour are influenced by mood-making chemicals or neurotrasmitters in the brain. Also four of these chemicals are produced directly from the food we eat. Protein, vitamins B and C, iron and magnesium are vital for these chemicals to do their job efficiently. Even to supplement these chemicals you have to eat leafy vegetables and fruits in sufficient quantity.

Techniques of tantropathy are developed in such a way that you can de-stress yourself daily. Today any discussion on health lies on the busy life styles of people with stress building up along with different responsibilities. Unless one takes the necessary measures to de-stress oneself, the risk factors also go up and leap eventually to a point of disaster. We have to allow some room for practising the techniques of tantropathy regularly and timely as well as diet as prescribed; then de-stressing comes automatically. Awareness of a good quality of life based on spiritual principles (not dogmatic religion) among the people is essential. They must target good quality of life within the framework of a busy and stressful working schedule.

Some short-cuts to relaxation

Modern living is full of stress and strain and suffering from killer diseases. Most people want quick relaxation either to get rid of dreaded diseases or to regain health, fitness and happiness. They use alcohol, smoking, chewing tobacco etc. Tantropathy (Tantra-Yoga therapy) suggests many short-cuts, which are simple but very much effective. It uses mind-body connection through asanas and mudras (poses and postures), specially Gyan-Dhyan mudra and Virasana Ruddh Pranayam, which help the mind and body to relax to the maximum. A simple method of relaxation is to give the body and mind a chance to unwind, be realigned, pampered, soothed and re-energised. Give them some time to recover and you will perform better. Above-mentioned mudras should be included in your daily routine.

- *Gyan-Dhyan mudra (Self unwinding pose):* This mudra can be called unwinding pose of mind and body. It works on the pressure points of hands, feet and whole body along with meridian channel of energy. You need only 5 minutes for this pose and all you require is a chair.

    (i) Open the palms of both your hands up to wrist, and stretch all fingers to maximum. Then bend middle fingers of both hands to touch the roof of the thumb and then the centre of the palm; repeat eight times and relax.

(ii) Open your ankle bones of both legs to maximum by stretching leg fingers and count 16 and then to eight and relax. It leads to stress-free position and calm the neurons from its confused and agitated state. Sit in Virasana, keep hands on thighs and visualize the colour, shape and Beej mantras of different plexuses for 3 minutes. From Muladhar chakra to Agya chakra colour, shape and Beej mantra are given below.

☞ *Angrai mudra (Body-twisting mudra):* According to tantra tradition correct stretching of the body dispels lethargy and energies of body and mind both. It is a great stress reducer. Light knotted muscles send uneasy messages to the brain, whereas relaxed

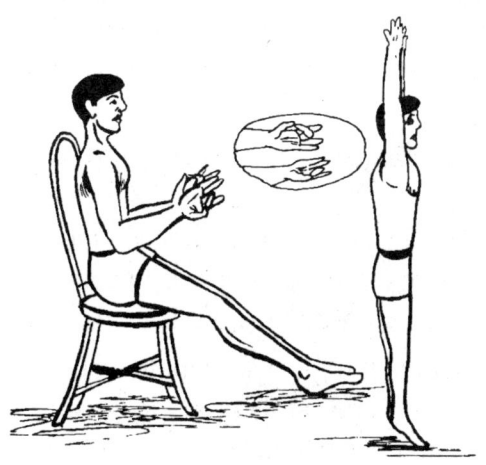

Angrai Mudra

muscles send all-well signals. You have seen that even animals like dogs and cats, after sleeping, take full-blown scream (Angrai) by stretching legs backward and forward and then standing on feet. Do not feel silly; who cares if it works for your fitness and health.

Have full-blown tantrum; a good Angrai scream by thrashing your arms and legs about, moving upper part of your body above the back to right and lower part of your body, before leaving the bed in the morning.

Open the wrist and ankle together by stretching fingers and toe to maximum and continue by stretching the whole legs and arms, touching the chair with back-raising hands up to head, and foot at 1 ft height from the ground. Repeat it thrice for total unwinding the mind and body.

☞ *Shubh Bhawana mudra (Positive thinking pose):* Lie down on your back, supporting your knee and head

Shubh Bhawana (Postive thinking pose)

on a blanketed floor or sit in a chair with your feet apart. Close your eyes, stretch lower eye lid maximum, leaning head slightly on the back of the chair with your hands on thighs. Take a few breaths with maximum length and think "I am relaxed". Then imagine that the sun is shining down on you from forehead to leg and warming from your right hand to whole body, as well as feeling of freshness, alertness and refreshment is coming within you. Repeat it in the same postures with your head leaning slightly forward.

☞ *Tatva Dharna (Visualization of nerve centres):* Tatva Dharna is a tantric process to visualize colour, shape and size and Beej Mantra from Muladhar Chakra to Agya Chakra in Virasana (Hero pose). Thus put the spine straight even in office or working place. Sitting on chair or standing you can take a full-blown angrai by twisting upper body from the navel first and then lower body from the navel in sequence and feel relaxed.

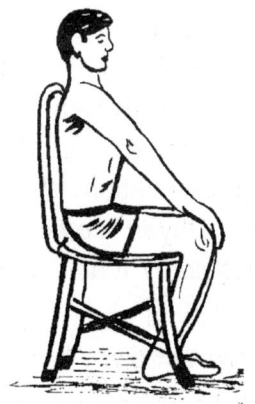

Tatva Dharna (Visualization of nerve centres)

Virasana Ruddh Pranayam (Deep breathing in hero pose)

Virasana Ruddh Pranayam is one of the cheapest and simplest and most instant processes for calming down the stress and strain within 2 minutes of its practice. Only you have to sit in hero pose, keeping hands on thighs and to inhale slowly and deeply from the bottom of your lungs. Feel your abdomen swell as you inhale, hold for a moment, then exhale slowly in your own time. The effect is immediate. You should know that success in life demands very high degree of physical fitness and mental alertness, more so when you are competing with diehard competitors. Just a small spell of fatigue during the working hour adversely shows up in your performance, so much so that you will be out of the race even before you realise it. Fitness on work implies an ability to get through the day with energy.

Isht Pranam (Process of meditation for meditation purpose)

'Isht Pranam' technique of tantropathy is invented and developed by the author after 20 years of experimentation. It includes postures and poses systematically and in sequence in three types of major poses: (i) Welcome pose (Abhinandanatmak Pranam); (ii) Half surrender welcome pose (Ardh Pranam); (iii) Surrender pose (Sashtang Pranam) along with the recitation of 'Om Namah Shivaya' rhythmically with the correlation of respiration. In this process Dharna and Dhyan come automatically with continuity, unity and regularity. It acts as natural tranquilizer for the practitioner.

The salient feature of 'Isht Pranam': This technique requires only standing in Tadasana posture comfortably in Indian traditional welcome pose (Abhinandanatmak mudra) for 5 minutes, involving eye movements with smiling pose (Prasanna Kriti) at the first stage. In second stage, practitioners have to sit in Virasana with straight spine, giving pressure on hips and lumbar region, bending hands from elbow, involving eye movement from left to right and right to left as well as from downward to upward and upward to downward. Then raise the arms above the head and touch the ground with palms stretching in Ardh Prana mudra. In third stage you have to lie down on the blanketed floor with abdomen touching the floor with sex organs of the body in surrender pose (Sashtang Pranam).

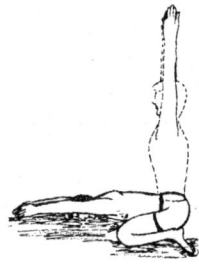

Ardh Pranam

Sashtang Pranam

Abhinandanatmak Mudra

You have to focus gently on something which has natural positive connotations to you, in surrender pose. The focus should not be on idea that can be thought but on something repeated, over and over a simple mantra — "Om Namah Shivaya" or even connecting that with your own breathing. Normal thought should not creep in occasionally, otherwise it will be total failure. It will be okay to leave it behind and continue as necessary in the morning for stress-free feeling for the whole day. For those suffering from ailments concerning respiratory, circulatory, glandular or nervous system, who must continue its practice for at least 3 months regularly in time. People who suffer from hypertension or heart disease are not advised to abandon their medicine without their doctor's advice.

Sweet water (sharbat) for relief of stresses and strain

There is an Indian tradition to offer a glass of 'Sharbat' (sweet water) to a guest. There is a proverb 'Muh Mitha, Man Mitha' (when mouth is sweet, mind is sweet). Sugar has been recognised as mood lifter in India and China both. That is the way we unconsciously reach for something sweet to change away blue mood, even with just a cup of tea or coffee or chocolate. Modern researches have found that sugar creates a feeling of well-being not because of taste but owing to its chemical effect on the brain. When sweet food enters the system, the body releases insulin to deal with sugar. Insulin also spurs the release of serotonin, a brain chemical known for its calming effects. Within an hour of consuming sugar, you feel tensed and slightly energised. But eating large amount of high-sugar food forms a false pick-me-up effect. To take sweets like pigfood may lift your mood for a short period only, to send it crashing a few hours later, leaving you more drained than before. The reason is that the load of sugar causes a rush of insulin into body. Over a few hours, this mops up your blood sugar so thoroughly that it leaves a feeling of draining and fatigued. To take something starchy, like rices will have the same relaxing effect as sugar without the big come down. Once you allow some room for regular and systematic exercises as well as well-planned and uniform routine and avoid hankering for food and other materials, de-stressing comes automatically. You should not forget that stressing is the outcome of running after food, not exercising regularly and not allowing the magnetism of the modern comforts of life, which drags you towards sedentary ways of life. Hence adopt spiritual way of life (tantric), which is really a quality of life within the framework of busy and stressful working schedule. If you are distressing yourself, start practising techniques of tantropathy, follow strictly the model daily routine and depend on natural (vegetarian) food.

By nature we really enjoy what we are doing. Tantra says, "Himmate Madda, Marde Khuda". We enjoy and feel happy by accepting challenging job, not by getting the fruits of efforts. Actually we become happy after getting the fruits of efforts temporarily, but do not make efforts for getting the fruits that give thrilling and timely happiness, which is the real source of health, fitness and happiness. By nature we really enjoy, what we are doing, when we have pondered over how much time and energy we spend in whining and brooding. This is apparently not because we actually have no time for ourself for following a model daily routine, but we are so engrossed in materialistic pursuits that we hardly have any time for relaxation. This in turn leads to stress and strain, and over a period of time this accumulated stress and strain leads to a host of ailments. We should not forget that stress and strain are the biggest group of killers in this world. The answer to this problem lies in practicing the techniques of tantropathy and not in allopathic medicines.

TANTROPATHY

GENERAL FATIGUE VS LIFE STYLE

Activeness is life and inactiveness is disease. People who are not engaged in hard labour like office workers often complain of tiredness and fatigue. Specially executives and housewives are surprised by how tired they feel all the time. When they go for medical check-ups to specialists they find nothing wrong with them. Be active the whole day and get rid of fatigue. Experts say that very often chronic fatigue has simpler origin, that is inactiveness. Working or living in a place that is plagued by inadequate light and air or too much noise can bring on fatigue.

All day fatigue could be an early symptom of anaemia, heart disease, jaundice and several other disorders. Working and living in unhygienic place can induce fatigue. Experts say that people who work in basement offices feel more depressed than others. Depression, anxiety, frustration, pessimism or feeling of overwhelmed by responsibility can bring on this kind of fatigue along with general aches and pain. In short a person who is psychologically worn out suffers from tiredness and general fatigue all the day. Some of minor things which are unknown to us, or we become unaware of, drain our life-running energy batteries more than we realise. Tension, thinking, lethargy, boredom, scrappy and irregular eating as well as scarcity of water in our body are the agents of fatigue and tiredness. Actually the general fatigue is the product of faulty life style.

Lethargic people are inactive physically and mentally both and feel more tired. Their under-used muscles become inefficient and feel overloaded with the slightest activity.

TANTROPATHY

Activeness creates a feeling of energy. Intensive thinking, which blocks out every thing else to focus on the task before you, takes more energy than we realise. A repetitive job often causes exhaustion. Housewives are particularly exhausted with the daily routine work. They might have plenty of energy to go shopping with friends. Scrappy and irregular eating leaves the people low on energy. They do not feel pangs of hunger as usual even if they get exhausted due to hunger. About 70% of our body is water and we need more water than the solid food. Body cells function best with a certain fluid content.

Preventive measures

- ☞ If you are an intensive thinker, it is a good habit for success but it should be time bound. Tantra says that energy activity of human-being from going to lavatory to sleeping or visiting temple is puja (worship). You have to perform your daily duty with a spirit of dedication and surrender. Forget every thing when you are performing daily duty with a spirit of dedication and surrender. When you are sitting in lavatory think only about movement of bowel, cleaning hands, teeth, throat, nose and the whole body. When you are doing exercises, taking meals or going to bed, think only about that particular job and thus you would have a good night, good morning and good day.

- ☞ Tantra says that every thing is moving and vibrating in this universe. Nothing is static in this world. Where there is static position, there is death and destruction. Hence activeness and dynamism represent life. To become lethargic is a suicidal life style. Those who are untidy, their belongings are scattered here and there in the room. Those who talk loosely are physically and mentally ill. Such people feel more tired and fatigued. They have to follow daily routine technique of tantropathy strictly, if they are really interested to get rid of this slow-poisonous disease. By following the model daily routine given in this book, you become active and develop a feeling of energy. Do use your under-used muscles to become efficient and feel energetic.

☞ If you are in service and feel boredom due to repetitive job and feel exhaustion, apply your mind to do something creative in the job. By doing so your creative work will be appreciated by your employer, and you will also get rid of exhaustion. Also practice Jamawant mudra morning and evening every day for 3 minutes only. Srijanatmak Manasik Natya Manchan (Creative Psycho-Drama Technique), technique of tantropathy should be practised for a few seconds daily and this will certainly help you to overpower boredom.

Procedure of Srijanatmak Manasik Natya Manchan: Imagine job-related persons — whether they are colleagues or co-workers or related persons — their mode of expression, talking, walking and habits, and mentally act and copy accordingly; you will immediately smile or laugh and relax. Sometimes you imagine the beautiful place that you have visited or the moment of your family that thrilled you with joy, to get rid of your boredom.

- Practice Isht Pranam and follow the daily routine given in this book, and after a fortnight it leaves you high on energy the whole day and you would feel pangs of hunger timely. We should not forget that we feel pangs of hunger, motion and sleeping timely every day due to habits formed after following certain healthy routine regularly.

- It is scientifically proved that more than 70% of our body is water content. We become tired mostly for want of proper level of water. Our body cells function best with a certain fluid content. On change in water level of the body, under low level the body sags and goes sluggish like an underwater plant. Hence take as much water as you can, at least 6 to 7 litres minimum daily and your tiredness and boredom would evaporate within no time.

- There is a tantric tradition in India to offer sweetened water to a guest immediately after welcoming him. Recent study shows that sweet is not only mood-maker but also a medicine for removing boredom and tiredness. For sweetish water, tea or coffee, a pinch of salt must be poured. It helps neutralise the acidity.

- Role of cold water in prevention and cure of tiredness and boredom cannot be ruled out. Water is life; we cannot live without water. It is just as vital to the outside of our body as it is to the inside. Only 25% in our body is solid bones and muscles etc. and the rest is water. Shortage of water level in our body affects both mind and body. Splashing the whole body specially face with cold water does not just wake you up when fatigue sets in, it is also great for freshening your skin, circulation of blood, giving it more colour and life. Always use cold water for bathing even in winter season and increase the span of your life.

We sometimes feel that we have lost all our "joie de vivre", the bubbling, almost child-like enthusiasm for life, that was so much a part of you in your twenty's that suddenly disappeared and has been replaced with cynicism and boredom as well as overwhelming sense of fatigue. But you should not fear. This attitude will not be a constant companion in the journey ahead. There is no way we can set things right; change your attitude. Do not look back, look forward. More importantly, look at present. All you need to regain what is lost is to start a few techniques mentioned in this book. If that will be done sensibly and in moderation, it would be enough for your fitness, general health and happiness.

☞ *Proper style of life:* Proper style of life forms the basis of actual health, fitness and happiness in the life of human beings. We adopt faulty style of life consciously or unconsciously under the influence of modern custom and culture in particular, and from our family members, classmates, colleagues etc. by auto suggestion, mass suggestion and prestige suggestion in general. We die from different diseases like arteriosclerosis, in which the arteries that carry blood to the heart are progressively clogged with faulty deposits until insufficient blood reaches the heart and the person has a heart attack. The only widely accepted cure of this dangerous disease is to increase the flow of blood through arteries by balloon or angioplasty or bypass surgery.

The age-old tantric culture of India expresses its heart through idioms, proverbs and simple sayings — 'Khush Raho, Swasth Raho', that is 'Be happy, Remain healthy.' Modern researches have also found that how life style changes can benefit the overall health of people in general and heart in particular. The value of humour in physical healing came into prominence when Norman Consens published the anatomy of an illness. He watched for hours films and video tapes of old comedies in movies and described, how after a good laugh, he felt less pain in the body. Laughter is a good medicine and it is true. Humour and laughter are increasingly recognised as sound counter-measures to the effects of stress and strain. You have to laugh and laugh till your sides burst or heart pounds and your eyes start watering and you will see that how your tension, stress and strains being washed out of your system.

Tantra says, 'Our feelings produce corresponding poses and corresponding poses bring similar feelings.' Hasya Kriti and Prasanna Kriti techniques of tantropathy bring feelings of heartiest happiness and even makes one laugh loudly after a practice of four weeks. Researchers have shown that our feeling, whether pleasing or depressing, positive or negative, are converted into neuropeptides or messenger molecules, which eventually influence every cell in our body towards health and illness or towards healing and fitness. When we laugh our positive emotions and feelings are converted into chemicals that prevent illness and heal diseases. After laughter, blood tests reveal that endorphins are produced, which act as a pain killer and our immunity increases. In the words of Mr Norman Consens, laughter is inner jogging. It is just like an exercise. It increases the rate, length and depth of breathing and

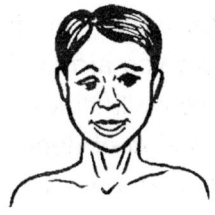
Hasya Kriti

Prasanna Kriti

exercises the abdominal muscles. Laughter creates a co-ordinated rhythmic movement of the muscles of the chest and face as well as massages the respiratory and abdominal organs including the intestines. This increases the secretion of various enzymes and improves circulation of blood. It decreases physical tension and stresses, and the feeling of happiness and relaxation sets in. Practice of Hasya Kriti and Prasanna Kriti techniques of tantropathy will induce a sense of appreciation and develop the sense of tolerance. These certainly would help you to become healthy, attractive and happy if included in your style of life.

The present style of life we have adopted by practice or by copying unconsciously or consciously. A new style of life has to be adopted only by practice of daily routine technique and Shubh Bhawana technique of tantropathy. Without changing life style it is not possible to get rid of general fatigue.

- *Keep happy, and look with shiny eyes:* In your daily routine 'Isht Pranam' is a must. It includes Jamavant mudra and Prasanna Kriti for facial exercises. "If you are happy, you are healthy; and if you are healthy, your eyes will look bright and shiny." "Dull eyes can be a sign of depression or stress", says Dr Barbara Bonner-Morgan of Anglian Medical Eye Specialist, Harley Street, London. If there are lots of yellow pimples under the skin of eyelids, it could indicate high blood cholesterol, increasing your risk of heart disease, whereas rings on your eye itself may also be sign of this. In this case switch to a healthy diet, cutting out saturated fats. Pull down your lower eye lid, it should be pinky-red inside. If it is pale, you may be anaemic. In this case see your doctor. Your pupil should be crystal clear. If that is cloudy, it may indicate early signs of a cataract, which can lead to blindness. In this case reduce its risk with a diet rich in antioxidants, vitamins 'C' and 'E', beta carotenes and selenium.

::::::::

CURE CONSTIPATION, HEART BURN AND HEADACHE THROUGH TONING UP OF ABDOMINAL AND RECTAL MUSCLES

We all are very much curious to know about constipation because we suffer usually from this commonest disorder of the alimentary tract. Though it is not dangerous in itself, it can lead to many other more serious disorders. What is it? What are its causes? And how it can be treated by techniques of tantropathy? These questions are usually confronted because appendicitis, arthritis, rheumatism, high blood pressure, cataract and cancer have all been linked to constipation.

There are three types of constipation and this classification relates to the causes of all ailments: atonic constipation, spastic constipation and obstructive constipation.

Atonic constipation

This type of constipation is most common and occurs due to lack of sufficient fluids in the diet. It is very prevalent in hot countries, specially in India in summer, when lots of fluid is lost through perspiration. The water in the colon gets absobed for use elsewhere, leaving faecal matter dry and hard and unable to provide enough movement of the bowels to facilitate their evacuation. It also occurs due to lack of roughage in the diet or not eating adequate fruits and vegetables and hence lack of bulk-forming cellulose.

The second cause is eating rich and refined food, drinking too much tea and coffee, which have an astringent effect. A frequent use of purgative which inhibit natural peristaltic movements, a lack of regular exercise of abdomino-rectal muscles (which causes weakness of the muscles) and a sedentary life style.

Spastic constipation

It occurs due to weak tone of the clonic muscles, deficiency of vitamm 'B' complex and lack of abdominal exercises. These are the known causes for a loss of tone of the bowel walls. Adequate supply of this vital vitamin and proper regular exercise will certainly lead to improvement over a period of time.

Obstructive constipation

It is usually due to malignancy of the colon, what is known as the impacted colon, and it may require surgery but certain techniques of tantropathy may be used before going for surgical treatment. The symptoms of severely constipated people include heaviness of head, insomnia, a coated tongue, foul breath, headache, dizziness and loss of appetite; in addition there can be mouth ulcers, acidity, heart burn and diarrhoea.

The remedy is not laxative or purgative to find an easy way out of this complex problem. These easy solutions may lead to chronic constipation. Even mild laxatives like milk of magnesia, isabgol etc. absorb a considerable amount of fluid and produce an irritating bulk. Purgatives lead to deficiency of potassium and this in turn affects bowel tone.

The remedy lies only with the practice of the techniques of tantropathy, which are given below in details.

Principle of the techniques of tantropathy

The principles behind the asanas and mudras are:

- To gear and to create a vacuum in the abdomen, thereby increasing the flow of blood to the area and making the organs and glands in the region work more efficiently.

- To flex and contract the muscles of the abdomen and rectum as well as of the visceca, and to generate energy by movement of abdominal cavity and pelvic cavity. Tantra advocates that abdominal muscles should be continuously massaged and should participate in the respiratory process. It will tone the area, prevent accumulation of fat and also aid respiration apart from improving circulation. The additional pay off is that you improve the digestive and excretory systems, which in turn improves most of the other systems of the body. The most beneficial technique of tantropathy is Isht Pranam. Isht Pranam has three parts: (i) Abhinanadanatmak Pranam, (ii) Ardh Pranam and (iii) Sashtang Pranam. Ardh Pranam and Sashtang Pranam are the beneficial postures and poses for strengthening the organs of abdominal cavity, which are given below:

    (a) Sit on a carpet or blanket in Virasana. Raise your both hands above the head and bend from waist and touch the ground. Stretch your hands and waist forward and give pressure of your body on heel and ground. Inhale deeply from the bottom of your abdomen and exhale normally with 'Aum' 8 times. Relax after coming again in Virasana. Repeat thrice.

(b) (i) From Virasana come to Chatush Padasana, and slowly giving pressure first on chest and then waist lie down on the carpet and stretch your both hands forward and both legs backward as much as you can. Inhale slowly and exhale with the sound 'Aum' 8 times. Repeat this posture of Sashtang Pranam thrice in the same style and manner.

(ii) Bring your both hands parallel to your waist, stretch hands and feet, raise your head from waist, bend as much as you can comfortably and fix yourself in that posture. Then raise your both legs by and by towards roof 8 times and again both legs gently, bending from the knee towards the roof 8 times. Then relax lying on carpet comfortably in the same posture. This is Salvasan mudra.

(iii) Catch your both heels with both hands from the back, raising head and legs up as much as comfortably you can do and stretch both hands and legs in the same posture. Move thrice, giving pressure on waist and chest, forward to backward and backward to forward, and then left to right and right to left.

(iv) Sit again in Virasana posture and do 'Sarpa mudra', twisting your vetebra from left to right and right to left 8 times and from upward to downward from waist and downward to upward 8 times.

Benefits

This technique of tantropathy corrects disorders of stomach and intestines and brings flexibility to hip joints. This will relieve constipation and strengthen the muscles of the back and the abdomen. This will also help regulate the bowel movements and control intestinal gases. It trims the fat around the abdomen and is good for heart, lungs, the back and abdominal organs. This will also improve the functioning of the liver, pancreas and the intestine in addition by making the spine flexible and lungs strong. This also controls the heart burn or an acidic burning feeling in the chest.

Note

Tummy on fire, a burning sensation in the pit of the stomach, can be a symptom of a peptic ulcer, particularly when it feels much worse after eating or drinking. There are two types of peptic ulcers — gastric and duodenal. With gastric ulcers the pain is felt about one and a half hours after eating, whereas with duodenal ulcers the pain is felt about two and half hours after eating. Around 10% of men and women are affected at some time in their life. If symptoms persist, one should consult a general practitioner (G.P.). If it is left untreated, an ulcer can perforate or bleed. We should not forget that occasionally these symptoms can indicate stomach cancer.

Above-mentioned techniques of tantropathy are well suited for abdominal ulcers and even cancer, if practiced regularly as given in this book.

Heart burn

Heart burn is known as acidic burning feeling in chest. We will discuss here its causes and remedy through techniques of tantropathy. Actually the fact is that the acidic burning feeling in the chest or heart burn sensation does not come from any thing in food but from stomach acids leaking upwards into the food pipe, whereas we believe that sour and spicy food going down the food pipe are causes of heart burn in the chest. But we often see that even taking sweets causes heart burn in some people.

Stomach acids are powerful enough even to burn skin, bleach the coloured cloth or remove paint. A tight valve normally keeps the acid in the stomach, which is built to withstand its action, by nature. But in certain conditions the valve fails, allowing the acids to creep into the food pipe. Here are some conditions that can derive the acid right through the valve, and that is overeating, wearing tight clothes, which are tight across the tummy, lifting heavy objects, or doing hectic exercises and lying in bed soon after eating a big meal.

Certain food, even non-spicy, can cause production of extra acid or loosen the valve. The usual offenders are coffee, tea, carbonated drinks, peppermint, chocolate, buttered or oily food, and heavy milk desserts. Anyone can suffer heat burn but it is commonest in overweight middle aged man, and pregnant women. Cigarettes, alcohol and erratic and untimely eating seem to make it worse.

TANTROPATHY

Some tips for prevention and cure

☞ Virasana Ruddh simple pranayam after taking meal. To stay after meal in Virasana helps hold the acid down, because human navel is the gravitational centre of the body, and though this technique of tantropathy acidic pressure is kept down the food pipe and the burning feeling is checked.

Procedure

(a) Kneel down on blanket or carpet, keeping spine erect by giving pressure on heels and keep hands on thighs. Without interfering in normal breathing, watch only the inhaling and exhaling. Do this practice only for 3 minutes after taking meal.

(b) Before taking meal, stand up with feet about 12 inches apart. Bend the knees and bring the back forward slightly, place the hand above the knees. Exhale fully from the mouth and, while holding this, push the abdomen in and out vigorously at lest 8 times without any discomfort. Then inhale deeply and relax.

(c) In another variation exhale from the mouth, push your abdomen in as much as possible and expand the ribs cage. The diaphragm should move up and abdomen should come in and look hollow. Hold this position for a few seconds, pushing the abdomen all the time. Then inhale deeply and relax.

TANTROPATHY

☞ There is a saying 'Ajirnasya Jalam Aushadhi', to drink water is the only effective medicine for constipation. Drink water before and after the meal to rinse acids out of food pipe and dilute the stomach acids. Before taking tea, coffee or soft drinks, you have to take a glass of water to dilute the stomach acid.

☞ You must lie down in bed after meal to your left side in 'Baba Shaiya', a technique developed in tantropathy. This Shaiya will keep your magnetic flow of body on right track, give your mind and body a soothing and comfortable feeling, and take proper care of passing gases from anus.

Procedure of 'Baba Shaiya'

(a) Lie down in bed on your left side, stretch your left leg and roll down your right leg heel over the knee of left leg. Touching the right knee, ring your left palm near the forehead and by adjusting your posture touch the Agya chakra with the last joint of the thumb and rest at least for 10 minutes in this Shaiya. Then take deep breath concentrating on the point where last joint of thumb is touched.

(b) The above-mentioned 'Shaiya' is only the rest pose. The proper sleeping shaiya is just reverse of this "Shaiya". Lie down in bed to your right side, stretch your right leg and roll down the left leg heel on the knee, right leg touching the left knee in the bed. Bring your left thumb near forehead, touch the eye-brow joint with the last joint of the thumb, concentrate on the touching point and adjust the posture in comfortable position. You will have sound sleep and good night's rest.

☞ Preventive tips:

(a) Drink water as much as possible and avoid any solid meals, as you can. (b) Eat small meals to avoid acid overflow after intervals of 2 hours.

(c) Do not consume unlimited antacid pills. It may block even normal acid production, giving you indigestion.

(d) If heart burn is worst when you lie down in bed or back, stretch your whole body by rolling down first from upper part of the body above waist 8 times and then below the waist 8 times and then raise the whole head left side of the bed by propping it on left hand. Roll down smoothly your right leg on the bed. Immediately some gases will pass out from the mouth and anus and you will be relieved from uncomfortable situation. This is Chakrasana mudra technique of tantropahty.

HEADACHE

What it is?

We all have an experience of headache and for that we consume so many Paracetamol and Analgin tablets without knowing what it is and how it can be cured? One of the functions of the brain is to feel pain, but you will be surprised to know that brain is itself insensitive to it. So a headache does not always imply a pain in the brain. In medical terms, it is called a nervous disorder caused due to congestion of the brain nerves and pressure on the blood vessels supplying fresh blood to the brain. The congestion or pressure is caused due to some impurities or toxins arising out of high or low blood pressure, anxiety, tension, fatigue, lack of proper rest and sleep, gastric trouble, constipation, indigestion, cold or sinusitis, strain on the eyes, excessive smoking or intake of tea or coffee or alcoholic drinks, a hangover or even due to use of tobacco. An overcontraction of neck and head muscles due to emotional or mental conflicts can also result in a headache.

Types of headache

There are various types of headaches. Some people suffer from chronic headaches called migraine, some get headaches only at a particular time of the day or only in one half of the head. Normally people use pain-relieving drugs to get rid of headache. But you must think of turning to the techniques of tantropathy to find out an effective alternative to these pain killers.

How it is cured

Techniques of tantropathy have the ability to relax your mind, flush toxins from every cell of your body and make you calmer. And as you become calmer, the frequency of your headache will drastically decrease, till it subsides all together;

- 'Baba Shaiya' technique: Get a good night sleep in 'Baba Shaiya' at least for 6 to 8 hours (as per details given in "Sleeplessness vs sound sleeping").

- "Isht Pranam technique": Practice Isht Pranam daily in the morning after getting fresh breathing (as mentioned under Stress Reaction vs Relaxation Response).

- "Virasana Ruddh Pranayam technique": Sit in Virasana (Hero posture), keeping your spine, head and neck erect; close your eyes lightly and relax the body and mind. Start exhaling slowly through the nose, at the same time putting your abdomen slightly more inside and hold for a few seconds, and then start inhaling slowly, stretching the abdominal muscles outwards. The expansion of the abdomen should be gradual and rhythmical and not abrupt. After inhaling for 5 seconds, start exhaling again. Repeat it 8 times daily. Note that Virasana Ruddh Pranayam technique is the abdominal breathing practice, which can be done at the time of evacuation in the morning in toilet room every day, sitting in traditional posture on pan for relieving constipation and accumulated gases in abdominal cavity.

TANTROPATHY

- Cleaning of hand, teeth and mouth and nasal wash by taking water from left nostril and then right nostril can be done at your convenience after throat massage with the help of index and middle finger of your right hand. It will remove all the dirt and bacteria-filled mucus from the nasal passages. It will have a cooling and smoothing influence on the brain activity and vanish headache and migraine after a few a days of practice, and hysteria, epilepsy and depression after practice for some months. It gives a general feeling of lightness and freshness in the head and subsides all the diseases of the upper region of the body.

- Bhut Shuddhi and Sharir Shuddhi techniques: Those suffering from chronic headache have to practice Chakra Shodhan-Bhedan technique twice a day regularly in the morning and evening. In view of its miraculous effect on the body and mind, it is called Chintamani mudra. It helps cure mental and physical problems.

Procedure:

(a) Lie down on back, with no thoughts in mind, with face upwards by keeping a pillow under the head. Or sit in Virasana or any Sadhan-asana with hands on thighs, spine erect and eye half closed. Try to see dazzling light on your forehead mentally, pushing the eyeballs within upper eyelids. Imagine that the circumference of light is becoming closer and closer and ultimately it remains a bright dot.

TANTROPATHY

It will take a few minutes to adjust, but after that it will work as analgesic, antipyretic and sedative. You may feel uncomfortable in the beginning but at last your headache will vanish. Practice this technique daily in morning and evening, before going to bed or leaving the bed daily, for a month at least.

Bhut Shuddhi

(b) Keep a mirror in front of you and sit in Virasana with hands on thighs, and stretch the scalp of your face and make Prasanna Kriti mudra. Stay for 2 minutes in that mudra and relax. Repeat it 8 to 12 times according to the severity of the pain. Then make Hasya Kriti mudra. Stay for 2 minutes and relax. Repeat 8 to 12 times.

(c) Massage yourself by making the figure 8 on your forehead, around both the eyes and ears 8 to 12 times.

TANTROPATHY

Procedure

Keep your right and left thumbs near right and left ears; the left index and middle finger above the left eyebrow, and right index and middle finger above on the right eyebrow. Try to make of figure 8 by circling ears and eyes while exerting pressure with fingers. Repeat 8 times and relax.

Sharir Shuddhi

(d) Lie down in Shavasana in Baba Shaiya and take a nap for an hour. It is medically proved that pain is diminished by relaxation and is increased by lighting up the muscles of that particular area.

::::::

TANTROPATHY
CONTROL OF DIABETES AND IMPOTENCY THROUGH TANTROPATHY

The restriction of certain foods and the moderation of total calorie intake are not the only remedies for diabetes, but proper exercise is also essential. In the initial stage of this disease it can be controlled by certain techniques of tantropathy especially designed for this disease. A common feature of this disease is excessive sugar in the blood and passing out of sugar with the urine of the patient. Actually whatever we eat is converted to glucose, which is the source of body energy. Insulin, which is released by the pancreas, reduces the sugar level, whereas glucogen and stress hormones, which are released from the body's energy stores, increase the sugar level. The cells of the body need a steady and regular supply of glucose in order to function effectively.

If the glucose level becomes too low, the cells starve; but if it remains high for a long period it can lead to infection, muscle wastage, heart attack, strokes, blindness or kidney failure. Common symptoms of diabetes are frequent urination, excessive hunger, excessive thirst, burning sensation during urination, fatigue, weight loss, constipation, impotency, diminishing vision, burning sensation in the hands and in the soles of the feet, giddiness and body tremors. Tantropathy looks at the causative factors and the techniques are designed to eliminate them, taking the energy from every nook and corner of the body and elevating the very immune system of individual by correcting and balancing the glandular secretion. Tantropathic system consists of particular postures and poses, technically arranged in sequence, rhythmically and in unity. It also uses yantra and mantra. But allopathy basically aims at suppressing the system by supplementing insulin in the body, which is against the nature because when there is supply of insulin from outside, nature will stop the supply from inside and the person may die in its absence.

What is required for controlling diabetes?

Stretching of back, twisting of spinal cord, retraction and locking of abdominal and pelvic cavities, massaging and toning up the organs of thorax cavity, and insulating and activating the chemicals of neurons are required. Adhah Urdhva Chakra Shodhan-Bhedan technique of tantropathy has been designed keeping all the above in mind, and positive result can be seen within a month after practising it (along with the following routine given in this book this technique is defined in detail in the first part of tantropathy).

Warning for diabetic patients

- ☞ They should avoid overeating and should take frequent small meals instead of heavy one. By doing this, the load on the pancreas gets reduced and it is easier for them to produce the required insulin.
- ☞ They should avoid fried, spicy, fatty and starchy food (rice, potatoes) and fruits like banana, mangoes and grapes.

Advice:

They should consume Amritann (sprouted gram, peas, soybean, moong and almond along with tomato, cucumber, and radish).

TANTROPATHY

☞ Patients should take citrus fruits like lemon and orange, and juice of bitter gourd and jamun or jamun seeds should be taken daily.

Note:

(i) The goal of a diabetic diet is do provide all of the nutrients needed by the body.

(ii) Vitamin supplements should not be taken unless specifically prescribed by your physician. In fact vitamin 'C' (ascorbid acid) in pill form may interfere with accuracy in testing of sugar in urine.

(iii) Insulin-dependent diabetics do not make insulin. When the body has no insulin and cannot use glucose for energy, it begins to burn fat. When fat is burnt for energy, acid wastes called ketones are formed. The ketones build up in the blood and cause a serious condition, called ketoacidosis. Hence those with insulin-dependent diabetes must take insulin to avoid this life threatening condition. This insulin must be injected. If it is taken as a pill, it would be digested and made inactive. Hence a balance of food, activity (exercises) and medication is the way to good management of diabetes.

(iv) Those with non-insulin dependent diabetes make some amount of insulin. But either there is not enough insulin or it does not work properly. This type of diabetes can be controlled fully if they practice the technique properly, timely and regularly every day and by limiting the type or amount of food they eat.

Impotency

The complaint of impotency is common in both ageing and young, but there is nothing to worry. It is often caused by poor circulation. The problem was discussed at Madrid at the International Conference on Impotency, by 900 Impotency Specialists. They were unanimous that in 60% of cases of impotency the circulatory problems are responsible. The vascular problems, such as heart diseases or diabetes are also related, and vasodilating treatments such as light exercises including those of pelvic region have proved very much effective. It can be averted by avoiding drugs, smoking and the abusive use of medication and alcohol, which can damage the nerves in the penis. Other causes of impotency, as stressed by Saenz de Tajada, President of the Conference on Impotancy, include the medicines taken for other illnesses, such as high blood pressure and depression, low hormone level and psychological causes such as anxiety, fear or shame.

If you are impotent, you have to change your life style first. Actually style of life is the life of human beings and those are health, fitness and happiness. You should not forget that you have invited this baseless disease by adopting faulty style of life under the influence of modern customs and culture in particular and from your family, class-mates and colleagues in general by auto-suggestion, prestige suggestion and mass suggestion.

Impotency is the product of our reaction to rejection,

lack of the sense of appreciation and tolerance at any time and by any person or working places at home, in conversation or in bed. If a sense of appreciation and tolerance is not developed, one suffers from fear phobia, which in later stage develops as impotency. Sense of appreciation and tolerance comes when we cultivate the habit of love and beauty with smile. The explanation of beauty is in its literal meaning:

      B = Balance between body, mind and spirit.
      E = Easy effective smile.
      A = Active and dynamic mind.
      U = Ultimate and optimum sense of humour.
      T = Trustworthiness.
      Y = Youthfulness.

One who keeps balance between body, mind and spirit, possesses enthralling smile, has active and dynamic mind and the ultimate and optimum sense of humour and is trustworthy and youthful, is a beautiful person. A beautiful emotion involves several components and is not a simple state that one can identify clearly for oneself by looking into a mirror. Interpersonal attraction is influenced by several factors and involves intense emotional state. Though love obviously means different things to different people, it consists of three major components — intimacy, passion and commitment. Regular practice of Prasanna Kriti and Hasya Kriti techniques of tantropathy will certainly induce a sense of appreciation and tolerance and remove impotency. Practice Isht Pranam technique.

TANTROPATHY

CHANDRAYAN TECHNIQUE FOR OBESITY

What is it obesity?

Obesity is the most obvious side effect of our lazy and affluent life style, though some consider "fat is beautiful". But we cannot deny this fact that it is unhealthy. Heart disease, high blood pressure, diabetes and tiredness are some of the ailments that are a part of the fat package. Obesity has drawn the attention of researchers world-wide these days and there has been a flurry of activity in the scientific community to somehow 'cure' this most obvious side-effect of our modern society. It damages the psyche of an individual, living in a society with unrealistic expectations. Researchers have been trying to understand the puzzles of obesity and they are of opinion that 'It is easy to gain but difficult to lose the extra pounds.' Even if some weight is lost by vigorous exercises and dietary control, it becomes harder for an obese individual to maintain the loss. There are two types of fat deposition in the body: (i) subcutaneous fat, the sort you can pinch an inch of; and (ii) the internal or visceral fat, which tends to accumulate around the liver and intestines. Males are particularly prone to the latter. If you do not keep the abdominal muscles in top class, this causes slag forward, making not only the paunch worse but also creating a hollow back and therefore back problems. The techniques of tantropathy more than just put it in shape.

☞ American researchers have been keenly studying the vital statistics of play-boy models over three decades and found that the contestants are now more than 13% below the expected weight compared with some one of their age and height.

It is found that 10 to 20% of healthy women's weight is fat, whereas for men it is only 12 to 20. Fat plays a vital role in reproduction and if the level of body fat drops below 15% in a woman, her menstruation ceases due to lack of enough oestrogen. Studies in other European countries have shown that it is more dangerous to be underweight that overweight. A major study in Norway showed that women described as plump live the longest, suffer fewer fractures, become more fertile and less likely to have heart attacks. The irony lies in the fact that men who have more to fear from obesity are under little pressure to shed weight, whereas women and girls, for whom obesity is a minor health problem, get obsessed and develop anorexia and bulinia. Doctors in America feel that we now have a distorted, absurdly unrealistic view of the ideal woman and that women feel guilty about being overweight by constant promotion of superthinness.

☞ In December 1994, 'Obese' gene in mice was discovered, which showed that mice, having an aberration in this gene were very fat, when the faulty 'Obese' was unable to produce a hormone, called leptin. Leptin is a Greek word, which means thin. Leptin is identified to be the satiety hormone, that tells the body when to eat less and burn more. When leptin was injected into plump mice, they lost 40% of their weight. But surprisingly researchers found that 'Obese' gene was normal in such people and an overdose of leptin that made overweight mice lose weight was in fact present in large quantities in obese people. Dr Jose Caro and his team at the Jefferson Medical College in Philadelphia discovered that the brains of the obese ignore the 'stop eating' message given by their leptin.

How can it be cured?

The reports of these researchers showed that they have not developed yet any solution to obesity. However, there is remedy of obese in tantropathy. Fat occurs due to many reasons like overeating, disorder of metabolism in human body, disturbed biochemicals in the body, impure digestion, enzymatic disturbance and glandular disorders. These can be corrected, regularised, improved and balanced by the practice of the techniques of tantropathy. There is a prominent saying in tantra, "Per Garam, Pet Naram aur Matha Rakho Thanda, es per bhi Rogi Kahe Vaidya to Maro usko Danda". It means that if leg remains warm, abdomen soft and head cool, then do not care even for the doctor.

Fasting is one of the oldest natural therapies in India. Fasting is called 'Vrata' in Sanskrit, which means puja (worshipping). Hence fasting without devotion and surrender is only keeping oneself hungry under compulsion, which has little effect or no effect; whereas 'Vrata' is puja (devotion), which directly affects central nervous system and corrects the disorder of metabolism in human body, balances the biochemicals and regulates the glandular imbalance. To keep healthy, one must always keep a little hungry. But unfortunately today we live in a culture of excess and under the influence of various spices, condiments and fast food, we gorge ourselves till we can eat no more. The food we eat provides our body with the necessary energy and enables it to produce new cells. Both these processes give rise to numerous toxins, which inhibit the efficiency of our body cells. Usually whatever we consume is first assimilated and this digested mass reaches the liver which, like the lungs and kidneys, extracts all the toxic or waste elements. As no new food goes into body during total fasting, no toxins are produced and liver works full time to eliminate the existing toxins. This occurs because the body requires food to survive. Now it begins to first burn the toxins to hinder cell functioning, as a result the natural resistance of the body increases manifold. The blood becomes purer and skin begins to clear and acquire a new glow.

In other words, when a person or patient stops taking food, the disease and not the person or patient dies of starvation. This aspect of fasting is well known in Indian culture, which is influenced by age-old tantra. There are three types of fasting prevalent in India — full fasting without food and water for 24 hours; fasting with liquid food as fruit juice, milk, curd or lemon water; and partial fasting as Chandrayan Vrata. Partial fasting is not modern dieting, it is ideal for even modern people.

Partial fasting

Partial fasting starts from the first day of moon (Pariba) with only one morsel of the choice food between day and night, but that should be strictly vegetarian. And after that, it should be increased to two, three, four etc. up to tenth of lunar day (Dashmi) and on the eleventh day there should be full fast. On twelfth day (Dwadashi) 12 morsels, on thirteenth day 13 morsels, on fourteenth day 14 morsels

TANTROPATHY

should be taken, and finally, on fifteenth day of moon (Purnima) there should be fast, using liquid (lemon water) only. Before taking meal, have full bath (Vyapak & Shouch), go to roof of your building, wait for the rising of moon, and perform Isht Pranam and have the partial food as mentioned above, but you can take prasad of Panchamrit (mixture of milk, honey, curd and ghee, and fruits) offered to moon in as much quantity as you can and go to bed. In the same way decrease the morsels after Purnima; 11 morsels on first day on (Pariba), 10 morsels on (Dwija) etc. up to tenth day, and on eleventh day (Ekadashi) have full fast and continue decreasing morsels up to 14th day and have partial fast on next days (Amawasya) perform Puja and then have full meal with your family.

It cures various chronic diseases (apart from controlling obesity) including anaemia, fever, headache, rheumatism, diarrhoea, gout, irregular menstruation and even depression. This view of tantropathy is confirmed by a recent study at the University of Pittsburgh, which found an increase in the activity of infection - fighting white blood cells in a group of fasting obese volunteers. Another study published over a decade ago had also noted that famine victims in Africa were less likely to develop malaria and T.B. than their better-fed counterparts in refugee camps.

The pay-offs of fasting are greatest in cases where the disease is deep-rooted, but, even if you are not suffering from any ailment, a fast for 4 days in each month specially on both the Ekadashis, Purnima and Amawasya serves wonderfully for toning up the system and increasing the body's natural resistance to diseases. Regular weekly or half day fasting (skipping an occasional meal) or juice fasting or fruit fasting all result in a tremendous improvement in the digestive process and the utilisation of nutrients. In tantra 'Chandrayan Vrata' is considered more beneficial physically, mentally and spiritually. It is also scientifically proved that from Ekadashi to Purnima, liquid things are attracted by moon and their flow becomes upward or reverse. Our body consists of 75% liquid and 25% solid. Hence for increasing immunity, power, confidence and will power, fast is essential. It increases stamina, accelerates weight loss and reverses the ageing considerably. However, fasting is not a solution of obesity. It is good way to start your programme, coupled with Isht Pranam technique of tantropathy, which will certainly help. During any type of illness, the metabolic efficiency of the body is in low gear and juices secreted are either improper or not enough. This is the way body reacts to fever with natural loss of appetite. Even birds and animals too instinctively suffer a loss of appetite when they fall sick.

Now modern people are realising, though slowly, that the body's wisdom is far greater than of mind. The Mind-Body theory further vindicates the benefits of fasting. It increases one's power of concentration and improves mental as well as spiritual strength such as will power, confidence, courage and peace of mind. All great men from West and East as Jesus, Moses, Mohammed Sahib, Buddha, Mahavir and all rishi, munis, yogis and tantrics of Indian culture have abstained from food in their pursuit of spiritual insight. Actually fasting is abstention, which forms the basis of truly spiritual life style, besides having therapeutic benefits.

Many among us try to keep fast but do not continue because they cannot control their hunger. But this hunger is craving of the mind than of the body. It is a subjective feeling, caused by the rhythmic contraction of the stomach wall, which goes on most of the time habitually and sometimes when stomach is empty. Each pang lasts from 30 second to 3 minutes and recurs in 15 minutes cycle. During Chandrayan Vrata fasting or simple fasting, these pangs do get more intense up to 3 days, but then automatically disappear. Before starting fast eat only light and nutritious food, preferably a large plate of salad and light meal. Drink at least 5 to 7 litres of water with lemon juice during the fast. In Chandaryan Vrata avoid physical work but you must do Isht Pranam in the morning after finishing morning duties and sleep in 'Baba Shaiya'. This serves a medium for carrying away the accumulated toxins. If you prefer, you can take water with honey also in Chandrayan Vrata. Indulge in the light mental activity as Bhut Shuddhi, Sharir Shuddhi and Mann Shuddhi; stay cheerful; take leave of haste and anxiety, and above all try not to think too much about food.

Chandrayan Vrata can easily be accepted in modern society, where people like to take something by habit without being hungry for 24 hours. Liquid things are permitted as much as one can. Even tea and coffee can be taken after taking a full glass of water. The human being is a sensitive, scientific, durable and very adaptable human machine created by nature. It gives a lot of signals to us to give some attention to it before it actually breaks down in the form of any illness or disease. What we would like to achieve here is to rise from our ignorance and laziness and perform Chandrayan Vrata.

Moon is respected in every culture because of not only its beauty but its miraculous effect on our body and mind. If ever you have enjoyed full moon-lit night sitting in a park or even in your lawn or roof, you will not forget that night. Buddhist monks concentrate on moon every day and do tantric kriya for spiritual development. This was one of their spiritual activities. To concentrate on moon, to take meal in moon-light, to watch the surroundings in moon-lit night especially in Sharad Ritu during winter and even perform Tantric Kriya in moon-lit night (especially in Sharad Ritu) are very much beneficial for physical, mental and spiritual health. Chandrayan Vrata technique is specially designed to take full benefit of moon power. A practitioner of Chandryan Vrata has to take meal in moon-lit night as per procedure, concentrate on moon at least for half an hour in Hero posture (Virasana) and walk and watch the surroundings in moon-lit night with smiling pose (Hasya Kriti) for a minimum of 108 steps while uttering 'Om Namah Shivaya'. Chandrayan technique is discussed in detail especially for obesity. It is very scientific and psychological and in this process the practitioner will also experience the magic effect of moon on body and mind. Actually we become habituated to take solid food more and liquid less, whereas our body requires 25% solid and 75% liquid diet as per one's constitution. When less solid and more fluid is given to the body for a month gradually with devotion and surrender to Moon — who is Chanda Mama to Children, Sasur (Chhatha) to ladies and Rajai (Priya) to gentlemen — our mind will be conditioned in that way and the sense of hankering for solid food would automatically disappear.

::::::::

CHAPTER 4

- Techniques of tantropathy 180
- Nirmimekh varjan technique 185
- 'Isht Pranam' technique 193
- Angari technique (hanging loosely) 208
- Prasanna kriti and hasya kriti 212
- Gyan-dhyan mudra technique 216
- Auto-suggestion technique in self hypnosis 218
- Meditation technique 222
- Model life style for health and fitness 225
- Good health is our nature 235

TECHNIQUES OF TANTROPATHY

In today's action-packed, stressful world, tantropathy advocates the idea that it is important to have peace with the self within the self. To achieve this, the first step is to be sensitive and perceptive towards all the senses with an alert mind, which is prepared to be alert to any findings. Actually man is a very sensitive, superscientific, durable and enough adaptable machine created by nature. We receive a lot of signals to give some attention to it before it actually breaks down in the form of any illness or disease. What we would like to achieve is to rise from our ignorance and laziness.

Nobody is perfect in this world but we can strive towards building the best physique for ourselves. A perfect physique does not mean perfect body measurements, nor the good looks. However, instead of paying attention to it every morning, we become ready to take on the worldly activities, though with good health we van survive with an energetic stride and a beautiful smile. The sedentary workers are more prone to blood pressure and heart attacks compared with those who take up regular exercise as a part of their life.

Fitness of any person can be assessed by judging his endurance level, present exercise level and the risk factor which he covers. Age, sex, family history, heart disease, diabetes are the factors that are out of control, but blood pressure, cholesterol levels (other blood chemistry levels), obesity, stress, alcohol consumption, smoking and apathy to exercise are the factors controllable by the techniques of tantropathy.

TANTROPATHY

The most important muscle in our body is our heart, which is hardly bigger than a clenched fist, pumping every second, every minute of our life. Appropriate technique of tantropathy can strengthen our heart too. Most of the people spend a great deal of time and energy worrying and fussing about different types of comforts about the body parts during the exercise and in return taking the heart for granted. You should not forget that when you are practising the techniques of tantropathy you have to concentrate only on the parts or functions of the body which are being exercised. The heart function is closely linked to lungs and the blood vessel network.

The heart is an automatic pump, which under normal resting condition pumps approximately 5 litres blood per minute, which normally returns to it from peripheral circulation. The response of the heart is proportional to the intensity, duration and time of work-out, and the most stressful condition for the human body is heavy and strenuous exercise. Actually the requirement of body tissues goes up to 20 times than normal with respect to oxygen and other nutrients, during heavy and strenuous exercises. Heavy exercise is most stressful for the normal circulatory system. During this, heavy flow in the muscles can increase as much as 20-folds. Techniques of tantropathy are based on poses and postures which are most suitable to our heart and lung fitness.

The duty of our lungs is to exchange gases. When we breathe in fresh air, oxygen is absorbed and while breathing out we expel carbon dioxide gas. Unlike the heart, the lungs have tremendous capacity for exchange of gases. An important point to be aware of is that all smokers have diminished lung capacity. The human body comprising a large mass of skeletal muscles can increase the total muscle blood flow to such a great extent that the cardiac output can be five times than normal. During heavy and strenuous exercises all the capillaries open up to maximum capacity, whereby even the dormant allowed increased blood flow taking place vehemently can wear and tear them and cause paralysis in the advanced age. Techniques of tantropathy are moderate whose exercises give soothing effect to smallest capillaries as well as protect and strengthen them.

Techniques of tantropathy provide strong muscular skeletal fitness. They involve muscles, bones, cartilages, tendons and joints, their functioning and their coordination, thus enabling you to maintain a good posture and bring about strong movements during sports like hitting a cricket ball or kicking a ball. These will also help you from avoiding injuries and muscle pain, strains, sprains, arthritis and osteoporosis. They can play an important role to build edurance, strength and flexibility for the joints. The back is most prone to injury in the muscular-skeletal system. We should not forget that there are approximately more than 400 muscles small, medium and large which function during our daily activities to sustain life. Obviously at birth the number of coils of the muscles are fixed but with gradual growth and advancing age they may improve or deteriorate depending on our use. Techniques of tantropathy take care of improvement and stop their deterioration.

Psychological fitness is our will power for achievement of confidence, determination, self esteem, desire, guts and the peace of life, whereas spiritual behaviour is our social aspect of life. All these help in building a fit mind in a fit body. By practising the techniques of tantropathy we should not forget that good nutrition is an important component of fitness, which should be assessed keeping in mind age, sex, mental status, exercise level and life style. Nutritional assessment should be gradually monitored as per body requirement, and the whims and fancies should be avoided us much as possible in choosing the items of food. Nearly two-thirds of our body is composed of water. Hence it plays a vital role in our life. Therefore fluid replacement and keeping the body well hydrated with electrolytes are extremely important. Positive thinking towards ourselves, family and society is spirituality fulfilling. It is our positive outlook as a whole and it comes by practising, forming a habit. It is Shubh Bhawana technique of tantropathy.

Long-term practice of the techniques of tantropathy is important in maintaining ideal body weight and muscle-mass as well as in decreasing the incidence of ill health. Many studies have shown that people who have high level of fitness have lower rate of coronary artery diseases and cancer. Conversely, sedentary life styles are associated with increased rates of arteriosclerosis and approximately 30% increased risk of death due to coronary disease. Practice of these techniques plays an important role in maintaining normal blood pressure and optimising cholesterol levels. It improve sugar metabolism also.

Low backache

Low back pain is one of the most common complaints in our society. We can blame it on a number of factors. But consider what you know and do not know about a fit back. Actually the most common causes of low back pain include sustained poor posture, incorrect lifting, incorrect bending or carrying and a lightening reflex of the erector spinal muscle group. Strong stomach muscles provide support for the back. Bent leg sit-ups, only curling to the middle of your back, keeping the lower part on the floor provide a safe exercise. You should flex the knees, tuck the hips and slowly reach down to your toes.

If you sit for more than 2 hours, get up and stretch; stretching and movement of back is essential for travellers, whether you are travelling by bus, train or flying. Avoid overweight if you have a tendency to back pain, because it increases the stress on the soft back tissues. Select a sound, balanced diet along with regular rhythmic and continuous low-impact exercise daily in the morning like 'Isht Pranam' technique of tantropathy, while pelvic tilt is effective for backache. Lying on back on a blanketed surface with knees bent, contract the abdomen, pressing small of your back into the floor, lift the buttocks with hips off the ground for a minute, and repeat it in reverse order. You will get a perfect score.

Sedentary individuals with abdominal fat, poor posture and improper diet are main culprits of backache. Shape up for your back's sake by regularly practising the techniques of tantropathy and stay fit for life.

::::::::

TANTROPATHY

NIRMIMEKH VARJAN TECHNIQUE

This technique is designed to solve a wide range of physical, psychological and spiritual problems. This technique is something more than modern hypnosis, which is an accepted way of giving up the habits that are detrimental to our health like drinking, smoking, chewing tobacco etc. Asthma, eczema, irritable bowel syndrome and high blood pressure can be treated by practising this technique. For that it is not necessary even to pay the cost equivalent to that for one consultation to enjoy the benefits. It can be easily learned and is very much effective for even general health.

Nirmimekh Varjan technique of tantropathy is neither hypnosis nor self hypnosis, but it is auto-trance. No doubt, auto-trance requires regular practice, and takes time and effort to see the positive changes happening within. Well-motivated and determined practitioner can achieve best result. To make things better, time and place should be fixed for the practice and there should be no interruptions, and sessions should be for 20 to 30 minutes each. Keep an alarm clock to limit the sessions. You can use your own bed-room but in a group will be more effective.

Procedure

Sit on a blanketed floor in Sukhasana. Keep both hands on thighs with crossed fingers, and keep eyes half opened. Perform body purification of physical techniques as given below. Relaxation of your body is essential and this technique will help you in this matter. As your skill in entering the trance state increases, you may reduce the time from 20 minutes to 10 minutes.

Nirmimekh Varjan technique

☞ Try to see yourself sitting mentally form head to toe and from toe to head thrice.

☞ Slowly tense the muscles of your feet and hold for a moment and gradually let the tension go.

☞ Continue working upwards through the muscle groups of the body. In the same way "slowly tensing and gradually relaxing" from toes, calves, thighs, buttocks, stomach, chest, back, hands, arms, shoulders, neck and face. Gently allow every muscle, every nerve and every fibre to become tense intensely and go slowly. By practising the technique you will have better control and you would be able to relax completely at your will through purification of internal body. In the same posture see mentally that you are sitting in an ocean and around you there is water and water only, and at far distance sky is touching the water. You are also hearing and seeing the roaring movements of waves of the ocean. Try to see every thing clearly in imagination.

Purification of mind

The aim of the technique is to develop a sense of fatigue and heaviness in the eye muscles and eyelids. Our conscious mind is expressed through our eyes first, then vocal cord and then muscles. Hence when eye muscles, eyeballs and eyelids also become heavy, automatically trance state of mind will be induced.

Look ahead, locate a spot above your line of sight on forehead and stare at it in the same posture. In this process your breathing will also become slow to an even pace. All these three techniques incorporate and work in unison. Its aim is to introduce the trance state by helping to develop a sense of fatigue and heaviness in the eye muscles and eyelids.

- *Tatwa Dharna technique of Tantropathy for relaxation:* For introducing a peaceful trance state, relaxed breathing, auto suggestion of calmness and muscle relaxation, adopt the following procedure.

    (a) Close your eyes in the same posture or Virasana and focus on breathing. Notice the rise and fall of your rib cage and imagine that the breath is a little cooler as you breathe in and warmer as you breathe out. Then focus on the rest of your body from toes to head and from head to toes, scanning it through all the joints and plexuses of the body thrice in one sitting. By this way allow tension to leave your body and muscles to ease and your relaxation to deepen, allowing the comfort you feel to seep gently through your body.

(b) Think and create first the location of sixth plexus — its shape, colour, test, beej mantra and smell, as given in the table from Muladhar chakra to Agya chakra gradually. On every plexus explore it, using all your senses — how does it look, smell and taste, the colour and sounds can you hear. Find some beautiful and comfortable place to sit, to enjoy the scene, and relax.

(c) Bring yourself out of the trance, counting backward from three to one and then open your eyes and stand up. Once you are in the trance state you can employ suggestive techniques to focus on your particular problem by moving 10 steps forward and backward. This can range from coming to terms with a fear or phobia to harnessing the will power to help yourself get free of any prolonged illness or ailment and to give up habits of drinking, smoking and chewing tobacco or lose weight. Medical disorders, particularly those with a psychosomatic ailment will be benefited from the use of this technique.

Eczema

In case of eczema, imagine a cooling ointment being spread on the affected area and that it is promoting rapid comfort and healing. Enjoying with the soothing sensation, notice in your mind the change of skin, becoming softer and more softer and normal in colour and appearance. Imagine improved flow of blood through the skin, which is providing extra nourishment for rapid healing. This can be done in trance, and, before you come out of the trance, suggest your mind that the comfort can remain with you till the another session at evening. Practice should be done in the morning and evening both till the symptom of ailment is removed completely.

Asthma

The technique described here is very much useful for asthma patients. It is preventive and curative both. Asthma patients are usually able to detect the beginning of an attack. Trance state of mind can help break the anxiety-wheezing, greater anxiety more wheezing cycle. During trance imagine a miniature fireman standing up in the centre of your way. Visualise him hosing down the wall of your bronchi, loosening and cleaning and loosening away the mucous plugs, calming inflammation and reducing the swelling. As you see this in your mind, feel your chest expanding more and more. Before you come out of the trance, visualise cool clean air rushing freely down the airways that you have opened up.

Note: Avoid trance state of mind if you have a history of epilepsy. Nirmimekh Varjan technique is derived from old text of tantra called 'Tratak'. There are three types of tratak — Dur (far distance), Najadik (closeness) and Antar (intro) Tratak. Nirmimekh Varjan technique is based on Antar Tratak. Far distance Nirmimekh Varjan technique is used only for the doctors who want to get occult powers specially for healing. These techniques will be discussed elaborately elsewhere, because for fitness and general health these are not required at all.

::::::::

'ISHT PRANAM' TECHNIQUE

'Isth Pranam' technique of tantropathy is universal 'Nut' for prevention and cure in particular and health, fitness and happiness in general. Regular practitioners of this technique must develop their physical, mental and spiritual formalities within a short span of time and should have magnetic, successful and pleasing personality. People may be interested in practising these techniques for losing weight, keeping fit or maintaining their proper shape, which is good, but the aim of this technique is to increase energy, vigour and vitality by stimulating various channels and plexus of our body, thereby keeping the vital organs in a good and healthy state.

(A) *Abhinandanatmak Pranam*

"Energy is consumed in thoughts". When we are tense, we think more and more and become more anxious, more and more fearful and more restless, and get exhausted. Thoughts are more repetitive, tiring and futile and cannot be put into action. Out thought is expressed through our fixed body channels — first eyes, then vocal cord and then muscles. Recurring thoughts in a tense state of mind can be checked in the morning by doing 'Isht Pranam'. The channels of vocal cord and muscles of eyes calm the tense and agitated mind and vital organs of head cavity, thereby making the body healthy.

Our five fingers represent five elements of Vishwa Brahmand (universe), and human beings are the living composition of these elements. These are Fire,

Water, Air, Sky and Earth. We become ill or suffer from corresponding ailments in unbalanced state of these elements. We receive or welcome an honourable guest or a nearest and dearest with folded hands, and that is thumb (Fire) with thumb, Index finger (Air) with Index finger, Middle finger (Space) with middle finger, Ring finger (earth) with ring finger, and Little finger with little finger. We press these fingers with each other and smile. This not only is a good gesture of welcoming but also to become healthy, fit and happy.

Procedure

Stand with feet 1/2 ft. away from each other, leg in Tadasana mudra (palm tree posture) in attention position. Stand before 'Shri Yantra' or a mirror and fold your hands in welcome posture with full bloom smile. Bring your arms by the side of your neck, stretching fingers and chest as well as

Abhinandantmak Pranam

lower eyelids maximum and look. Raise your arms above your neck, smile while extending the upper eyelids maximum (with smile). Then fold your hands, press fingers with each other, bend that from elbow and touch Agya Chakra with thumbs first and then Vishuddh Chakra. Stay for a few seconds and relax. Repeat this thrice.

(B) Ardh Pranam

There are two types of energies in our body with which we are born, whose constant flow is maintained by eating, dreaming, breathing and exercising. It is even preserved through practising moderation. To build and generate this energy is in our hand by practising Isht Pranam for maintaining health and vitality by doing away with any blockage or depletion. There are four channels of energy — large intestine, lungs, heart and small intestine, and lower abdomen. Ardh Pranam is the technique of tapping the energy through these channels.

Procedure

After practising Abhinandanatmak Pranam, sit on left leg with folded hands, stretch lower and upper eyelids to maximum and lock. Move both eyeballs to left as much as possible and then see the point in front of you. Repeat it eight times, then sit on both legs in Virasana in same pose and move eyeballs from extreme left to right and left to right and repeat it eight times. Again sit on right leg with folded hands in the same pose. Move eyeballs to extreme right side and fix in front. Repeat 8 times. Then sit on both legs and move eyeballs from right to left and left to right 8 times. Then raise your hands beside the neck, bending from elbow, stretch your lower eyelid, see the knee by moving only eyeballs and then front point. Repeat it eight times. Then raise your hand above the neck, stretch your upper eyelids and see the roof of eyebrow by moving eyeballs only and then front point. Repeat it eight times. Then fold you hands, touch your Agya Chakra in Abhinandanatmak mudra then Anaahad Chakra.

Sit in Virasana, bending your knees in such a manner that the soles of both feet touch each other. Sit straight, then straighten your back,

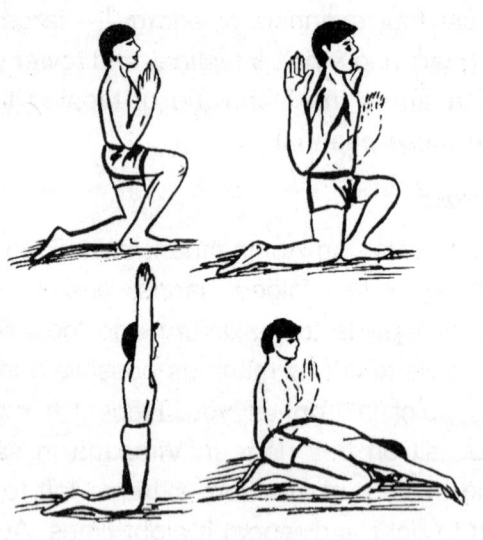

Ardh Pranam

bring both hands on back, intercross your fingers, and stretch first. Then grasp your toes with your hand, pull your feet as close to your hips as you can, and then raise your hands above the neck and bend from your back, touch the ground and stretch; repeat it in the same manner thrice. The technique will work miraculously on large intestine channel, lungs channel, and heart and small intestine channels.

(C) *Sashtang Pranam*

Every time there is an intake of food by the stomach, the vagus nerve, which is a part of the parasympathetic nervous system, becomes active and makes the stomach secrete juices in order to digest the food. These juices are highly acidic in nature. The vagus nerve also triggers this secretion when you are under stress or are in emotional state of anger or jealousy. This could easily damage the lining of the stomach walls. This condition when there is excessive gastric juice in the stomach is called Hyperacidity.

Sashtang Pranam

The health of the stomach is maintained by a very delicate balance in the quantity of acid in stomach walls. The mucin coat protects the stomach wall form the acid. Any imbalance in it can lead to stomach disorders. Actually stress is the main factor for hyperacidity, as it makes the vagus nerve hyperactive. As a result, a high quantity of acid is produced, which disturbs the balance. Stress also affects the blood supply to the stomach walls, which in turn affects the quantity of the mucous coat, making the stomach wall more vulnerable to the acid. Hyperacidity could be also due to sedentary habits, lack of exercise, eating at irregular intervals or eating high quantity of spices, sweets or fired foods. 'Isht Pranam' will help in calming the nervous stimuli to the stomach and improving the blood supply to the stomach wall, thus ensuring a healthy balance in the stomach.

Effects on body

Sashtang Pranam is the third state of 'Isht Pranam'. Practice of this technique makes the blood flow a little faster than normal to enable the active muscles to get a good supply of oxygen. By this way you let the muscles know what is coming, and by signalling them they are better prepared for the work ahead. The joints and ligaments need to be lubricated by moving them through a full range of motion, and that is done in this technique. This technique also warms up the whole system of the body, which also improves the neuromuscular co-ordination, that allows the message from the brain to pass on to the working muscles more quickly and effectively. It increases the core temperature of the body, which is more important because warm muscles lengthen and shorten better than the cold ones.

Our body is made up of living cells and tissues which are not elastic like rubber. Hence muscular ability to bear stress and strain depends on your general health, stamina and endurance. Free hand exercise or resistance exercises, done as per your own body weight, pass all the acid tests. Hence exercising with modern equipments lays undue stress on muscles, which could lead to irreparable damage to muscle tissues and you may end up with long-lasting back pain and other spinal injury. Push ups, pull-ups and squat are very effective for building muscles but they badly damage the capillaries, which leads to problems in advance age.

Principle behind the technique

The principle behind Isht Pranam technique, which comprises Abhinandanatmak Pranam, Ardh Pranam and Sashtang Pranam, is to gear up and create a vacuum in the abdomen and pelvic cavity, thereby increasing the flow of blood to the area and making the organs and glands in the region work more efficiently. Besides, they also help flex and contract the muscles of the abdomen and those of the viscera and generate energy by movement of abdominal and pelvic cavity. Tantra advocates that the abdomen muscles should be continuously massaged and should participate in the respiratory process. And for that the breathing (inhaling and exhaling) should be from the bottom of the abdomen.

By practising 'Isht Pranam' you can feel young for ever, even in advanced age. A child is supple and agile because of his flexible spine, joint and muscles. He can move in any direction easily and comfortably. As he grows older, his body gets more rigid, and the agility levels decrease abnormally with it. Ageing process can be delayed by maintaining flexibility of spine, joints and muscles of the body through the techniques of trantropathy. Tantrics have found that one can halve the ageing process by keeping the spinal cord flexible. A flexible spine will keep a person agile, young and his nervous system active. Sashtang Pranam is unique for keeping the spine flexible.

In Sashtang Pranam the spine gets laterally stretched up to hips, which increases its flexibility, improves the functioning of the lungs, heart, liver, stomach and intestines. It maintains the elasticity of spine and also exercises arms, shoulders, waist and neck, making them flexible and supple. It also increases the blood circulation in the body and has positive effect on the abdominal and pelvic cavity. It maintains vigour and vitality by doing away with any blockage or depletion of every part of the body. As explained earlier there are four channels of energy in our body. These channels of energy are associated with respective organs, and when this energy is pressed along the length of channels it passes through a problem area. The flow of energy is stimulated by practising Sashtang Pranam. This helps the organs without actually touching them and keeps the part of the body in good condition.

TANTROPATHY

Tantra says that there is an establishment of Pran within our body, whose virtues, functions and effects on our body and mind are narrated in detail in tantric texts. Now modern scientists are also accepting the establishment and existence of Pran, calling it conscious energy. Light, heat, magnetism, electricity and sound are the types of energy. What is in the universe, is also in the unit (body). Modern science considers human mind, heart and eyes as electric energy-generating centres and sources of flow of conscious energy (Pran) in our body. E.M.G. is used in case of inactiveness and paralysis of the body. Sashtang Pranam activates the centres of conscious energy and makes the practitioner energetic and jubilant for the whole day.

Procedure

- Sashtang Pranam is the divine welcome mudra, in which all the eight parts of the body — both legs, abdomen, chest, both hands, chin and forehead — should touch the ground. Stretch both hands above the head, touching the ground, both legs backward in the same manner. Sashtang Pranam is the third stage of Isht Pranam. It should be done just after doing Abhinanadanatmak and Ardh Pranam thrice. (a) Bring both hands by the side of your back and by giving pressure on both arms raise your body above the navel. Then raise the left and right legs gradually towards the roof eight times. After that raise both legs towards the roof eight times in Salva mudra and relax. (b) Grasp hands and feet to maximum and make Dhanush mudra by rolling the body in the same posture slightly left and right eight times, and relax. The a and b parts of this technique will tone up the abdominal muscles and buttock muscles both. (c) Salve mudra tones up the buttocks. Our buttocks have three large gluteal muscles — glutens maximums, glutens mediums and two glutens minimum. It establishes the hips and keeps muscles in alignment. This results in better posture and protection of the lower and middle back from strain. Buttock toning begins with simple clinching exercises.

☞ Nawaka mudra tones up the abdominal muscles and gives shape to flat stomach and improves body shape and posture as well. The muscles of the abdomen attach the upper body at the ribs cage with the lower body at the pelvis and serve as a bridge between the two, holding the spine erect in its natural position. They work in unison with the back muscles. So while working hard at the abdominal level, remember to exercise the back muscles as well. The mid-section of the body is primarily made us of these two muscle groups. There are not many bones or ligaments. Hence it is vital to take good care of the muscles.

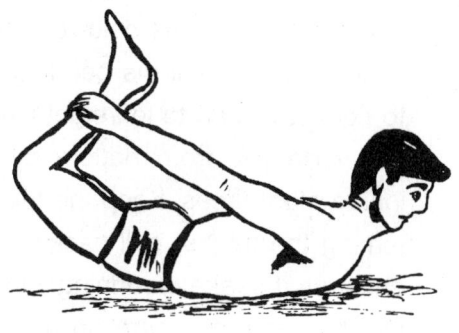

Four different types of muscles make up the abdominals, starting with the innermost layer called "the transverse abdominis" that runs horizontally, surrounding the waist and holding the organs in this cavity. Next is called 'Internal obliquus' which run diagonally starting from the pubic area of the ribs, followed by 'External obliquus' which run opposite to the internals. These two groups together help you to twist and turn and move your waist from side to side. The topmost layer is the rectum sheath, that runs straight from the pubic region to ribs, divided by the livia alba. These muscles help you to bend forward when you want to pick up something from the floor. Isht Pranam exercises all these muscles properly, rhythmically and systematically. Sit in Virasana, folding legs from the knee and sit on ankle, giving pressure on hips. Keep muscles relaxed, shoulder pulled back and down, spine centralised by ensuring that the muscles of both sides are equally balanced, and arms held relaxed by the side, slowly move the arms bending from from left to right and right to left eight times. Then twist the vertebrae from bottom by pushing hips inside eight times. Keep the tail bone lifted by jerking the thighs, pull backward and forward chest as if snake is running, standing straight. Do the same to warm up arms, arms joints, elbow joints, wrist joints and finger joints of both the hands. Stretch the face scalp making Hasya Kriti by movement of eyebrows. Massage the ear, nose and head, because their cavities are joined with ligaments. Then slowly move the head from side to side as if you are saying a big 'No'. Then take the head down and let your chin touch the neck line and bring it back to the centre as if you are saying a big 'Yes'. Take the right ear to touch the right shoulder and bring it back to the centre. Repeat the same on the other side slowly 8 times each with same stance as above and make small circular movements with shoulder joints from left to right and right to left. Repeat it 8 times.

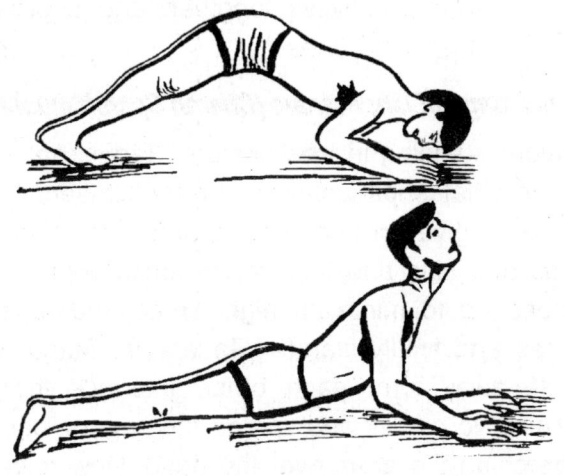

We should not forget that the technique makes the blood flow a little faster than normal to enable the active muscles to get a good supply of oxygen, and by this way letting the muscles know that it is coming up and there by signalling them. They are better prepared for the work ahead. Joints and ligaments of vertebrae are lubricated by moving them through there in full range of motion. This technique warms up muscles, organs and different systems, which would also improve the neuro-muscular co-ordination. It means that the message from the brain is passed on the working muscles more quickly and efficiently. We can call it rehearsal for the whole day activity. Initial warm up techniques of tantropathy increase the core temperature of the body, which is most important because warm muscles lengthen and shorten better than cold ones.

(D) Final stage of Isht Pranam (Charan Sparsh mudra)

Before standing in tree posture (Tadasana) you have to do Chatushpadasana just after Virasana. First you have to give on both hands and feet, then on both legs and hips and then try to touch your toes, bend knees up to minimum eight times and repeat eight times and finally stand in Tadasana. Stand with legs 1 ft. away form each other, interlock the thumbs behind your back and spread the fingers, bend down, stretching the arms over the head. Now release your breathing and try to hold this position as long as you can. You will tab the energy from large intestine channel by this way.

Then stand and step forward on your left foot and keep the toes of your right foot on the floor for leverage. As you do this, inhale and simultaneously stretch your arms up and out, stretching your fingers to the fullest. Look up to the ceiling as you hold the stretched pose, retain your breath, exhaling slowly, come back and relax. Repeat on the other foot and do this eight times on each side and you will tap the energy from lung channel by this way. For tapping the energy from heart and small intestine channels as well as lower abdomen channel, do "Tandava Nritya" only for a minute or two.

Procedure

Keep your legs 1 foot apart, spread your arms beside your chest and jump so that right leg spreads left side touching over navel. Keep spine straight, then again jump so that leg spreads to right touching over navel. Continue for 1 or 2 minutes and then relax.

Sankochan Prasaran mudra (Auto pressure or self massaging technique)

Auto pressure or self massaging technique of tantropathy is actually the pressure for pleasure. In massage technique we use the power of hands, palms and fingers along with Dharna (contemplation) of that particular part of the body during the massage and we really enjoy divine pleasure by doing that. In case of headache, making English figure by movement and pressure of fingers of both the hands covering all eight sinuses of the facial cavity (forehead-2, eye-2, nose-2 and ear-2), and visualising these pressures mentally is a unique experience.

You can keep the scalp and hair in good working condition by massaging regularly with or without oil or cream. The movement of your palm and fingers will act on the blood vessels beneath the surface and on the hair follicles, increasing the blood supply to the whole area. By pulling lower and upper part of the ear by catching with your thumb and index finger and applying pressure on the top of your head with middle finger, you will raise your energy as well as balance the emotion. In India, parents and teachers balance the emotion of kids by pulling the ears, but they do not do it properly. They use balls of fingers of their both hands, applying as much pressure as comfortable and relieve tension at the base of the skull by encircling thumbs and fingers along the hair line. You can use vinegar or lemon juice with coconut oil for massage.

Forehead, eyes, cheeks massage: To appear more expressive on your forehead, to increase the horizontal rows, practice Hasya Kriti and Prasanna Kriti techniques as much as you can along with Swan, Shukar, Vyaghra and Hasti mudras. This will stimulate circulation to the forehead by the us of small pinching movements of scalps. Also massage with your palms from left to right and right to left ears. There is a saying that the lighter the waves of eyes, the better is the ability of an individual to throw off diseases. Your vitality, emotions and general health are reflected from your eyes; though the eyes may appear fairly robust the skin around them may not. It needs special attention. Jamawant mudra perfectly works along with massage of eyelids lightly with middle fingers of both hands. Beneath the muscles of the cheeks lie a series of hollows that can become the dumping ground for waste, fat and lymph, and accumulation of these distorts the natural shape of the cheeks. For this massaging from both palms in a circular movement from ear to chin daily in the morning before leaving the bed along with following Mantra is very beneficial.

        Karagre Vasati Laxmi |

        Kar Madhye Saraswati | |

        Kar Mule Basey Govinda |

        Prabhate Kar Darshanam | |

The neck and shoulder are one of the first areas to show the signs of ageing. These are the most graceful and hard-working parts of the body, and the tension stored in the neck muscles undermines the health of the tissues there. You have to protect the skin of the neck from dehydration and environmental damage and for that have to practice tantric mudra technique. Isht Pranam includes all these mudras.

::::::

ANGRAI TECHNIQUE (HANGING LOOSELY)

Angrai technique is developed to stretch out the whole body and remove the feeling of stiffness, lethargy and feeling of minor aches and pains. It energises the body and mind both. The modern life is full of tensions. Even desk work and limited activity can leave you stiff than you know, and even in the morning when wake up you feel drowsy, fatigued and depressed. You feel better if you stretch the whole body through "Angrai technique of tantropathy". This type of fitness can improve your stamina, if you do a few times daily. Angrai technique is definitely a great stress reducer and useful in modern days. "All well" signals are sent by relaxed muscles to the brain, whereas tight - knotted muscles send "Ah! what to do now" signals. To run the life train properly, Angrai is the green signal that you have to flag.

Hang loosely and get on in whole-day activity. You will be surprised to know that if you are depressed, you are less likely to succeed what you are doing. To work efficiently and to become successful in life is a simple case of demand and supply. As we know that work requires energy and only a certain limited amount of energy is available daily to us. When one is tensed, muscles become taut and rigid, and activity with tight-knotted muscles uses our energy beyond our expectation. Hence the amount of energy available for day-long work is greatly reduced. A noted psychologist William James said that it is a relaxed and easy worker who works most efficiently. Tension and anxiety mixed all at once in the mind only drag the people in reverse gear, and create hindrances in speedy progress to success. The fact is that most of us today tend to live too much in tension and endure too much of a nervous strain; in that stage how we can be productive? Tension and emotion are closely related, and in such situations we tend to grow nervous, anxious and over-burdened. Then we should keep our muscles loose deliberately and nerves unstrained. Certainly by doing this, fearful, anxious and foreboding attitudes will be reduced and through the practice of Angrai technique it can be inhibited and prevented altogether at least for the whole day.

You have seen people work themselves into a state bordering on muscular spasm when waiting for a bus or train or plane or attending business interview, and even in attending lectures or concerts their seem to be listening with their bodies rather than with ears. They lie tightened up and rigid in sleep. This is the reason that working women and writers develop cramps through unnecessary muscular contortions. It has been medically proved that cramps and pains are diminished by relaxation. To overcome it follow the points given below: (a) Give maximum thought before taking any action, and when action is over do not dwell on the wisdom of it. Keep in mind that you have no control on success or failure both and worry for that would not change things. (b) Save energy by using only those muscles that are actually required. There is no need to tighten the whole body. (c) You have capacity to do so many things but assign priorities and cut down that which is not absolutely necessary. (d) Take deep breath from the bottom of abdomen and at the same time fill your chest and simultaneously distend you abdomen when exhaling and slowly pulling your stomach in. (e) Practice

Angrai technique a few times daily as and when you feel sluggish, lethargy or stiff.

Procedure: Angrai technique means stretching the whole body in Tadasana or Shavasana and at the end full - blown tantrum. Stand in Tadasana or lie in bed in Shavasana. First take a few deep breaths from the bottom of the abdomen. Throw your legs and hands with movement of your body above the navel left to right and right to left. The lower portion of the body below the navel should move in opposite direction slowly. Simultaneously stretch the hands, opening palms, fingers and legs, opening toes and ankles from each other. Lightly clasp your hands behind your head and push both the elbows backward. If you feel little stiffness in your shoulders, you needed that stretch.

Neck, shoulders and back are the stiff spots that make you feel tired at work. Most people do naturally when they get up. "Standing on toes, stretching upward and out" is good enough for starters, but beware of stretching the body unnaturally. Safe stretching is gentle and slow. There should not be backward bending (for beginners), jerking or twisting, teeth clenching or breath holding at any stage. Stretch only till you feel resistance. Pain is the signal to stop. As per tantric texts, stretching while breathing with right nostril will calm the spirit. Breathe out gently as you stretch and hold the stretch for minimum 30 seconds.

Today everybody wants to look trim and not strong, but everybody hopes to remain mobile and free of aches and pains. That kind of fitness needs flexibility, which many people lack even in youth. Stiff joints and muscles may not be obvious in the early years, but may show up in

Angrai Mudra

young people when they are reluctant to do physical work and feel tiredness. The stiffness shows up as pain in moving around and difficulty in doing one's daily chores. Jogging, walking or sports keep you fit in different ways, but the secret of a smoothly working body is stretching. Angrai technique is simply stretching all joints and muscles in all their natural direction — up-out and forward keeps them fit, relaxes muscles, improves circulation and makes physical tasks seem less tiring. It will be best to start on a flexing routine before the body stiffens. It can be started at any age. This technique is must for the people with sedentary life style.

TANTROPATHY
PRASANNA KRITI AND HASYA KRITI

Tantra says "Mudra changes our emotions, intellect and volition". Actually we are very poor to survey our inclination and thoughts, words and actions. We only become aware of their effects when we suffer. Effects are recognised by corresponding bodily changes, poses and postures. When we are in any trouble, our bodily poses and postures change accordingly. Then we express sorrow or repent. It involves three elements — change of mind (intellect), change of body (emotion) and change of will (volition). In the same way corresponding mudras and postures bring changes in all these three aspects or elements. "As your mudra is, so you are", is a prominent saying of Indian rural-folk and it has scientific background. Prasanna Kriti and Hasya Kriti are such techniques of tantropathy which give positive green signal. "All well, go ahead".

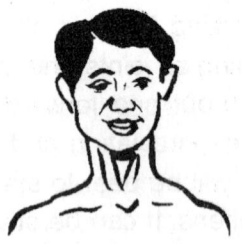 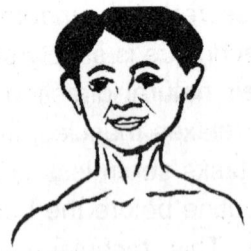

Hasya Kriti   Prasanna Kriti

TANTROPATHY

The tantra techniques of Hasya Kriti and Prasanna Kriti have positive impact on various parts of the body. We know that our mind is expressed through three body channels — first it peeps from our eyes, then is expressed from vocal cord, and then it reacts through muscles. In Prasanna Kriti all these three channels are utilized to produce positive thoughts, feelings and emotion, and induce and enhance the volition. This technique is an associate technique of Isht Pranam, which involves raising hands up towards the sky with opening chest and stretching body and coming back to Abhinandanatmak mudra. In this technique scalp of the whole face is stretched to the maximum. Fixation of eyelids and movement of eyeballs and uttering of Shubh Bhavanatmak mantra, involves all three channels and makes the precautionary person feel less inhibited. It is a boon at the time when life is very stressful, and the diseases related to sheer fatigue through coping with everyday pressure are on the rise. High blood pressure, anxiety, depression, nervous breakdown, heart diseases, peptic ulcers are some of the examples.

The benefits can generally be attributed to positive thinking. It strengthens our immune system. As per psychoneuro immunologists, "all negative emotions weaken the immune system and this technique raises the body levels." Certainly the frequency of common colds, sore throats and chest infections and abdominal disorders can be reduced if this technique is practiced regularly in the morning. It is proved that it increases the level of endorphin, which is a natural pain killer. It gives relief from asthma and bronchitis. It improves stamina and day-to-day performance. Techniques of tantropathy are not just exercises but are more than that. They actually make you more creative, boost the mood and bursts of creative thinking.

The age-old tantric culture of India has been expressed through proverbs, idioms and simple sayings. There is prominent saying that if you are happy, you are healthy. Laughter is a good medicine and it is very true. Laughter and humour are increasingly recognised as sound counter measures, especially to reduce the effects of stress. If you laugh, laugh till your sides hurt and your eyes are watery; you will see how your tension, stress and strain are being washed out of your system. It can help you even in regaining the lost health. But humour and laughter are not so easy, keeping in mind the time, space, and person. But practice of Prasanna Kriti and Hasya Kriti techniques is most easy for all groups of people and produce the same positive feeling within a few seconds.

Researches have shown that our feelings whether positive or negative are converted into neuropeptides or messenger molecules, which eventually influence every cell in our body towards health or illness. When we practice Hasya Kriti and Prasanna Kriti, positive emotions and feelings arouse and are converted into chemicals that prevent and heal diseases. Enough endorphins are produced, which act as pain killers and develop immunity. It creates a coordinated rhythmic movement of the scalp and muscles of the face first, and then convert and colour all other movements of the body during the period. This increases secretion of various enzymes and improves circulation of blood.

In a world where appearances matter more and more, it is the face that can launch a thousand ships. At the central point of the face is the mouth. You cannot maintain your impression and magnetic appearance only with cosmetics. It needs proper massage of the muscles of face as well as adequate exercises, and for that you have to take proper nutritious diet and practice. We should not forget that it is not just the teeth that smile, but it is the mouth, the eyes and the entire face. Regular practice of the techniques of tantropathy affects the mouth and produces such pleasing effects that would change the entire personality of the practitioner and bring a sparkle to his eyes, and you will be able to flash "50-year-old smile into 30-year-old smile". Actually the technique of Prasanna Kriti and Hasya Kriti are meant for personality enhancement.

Nowadays things are changing especially with the booming television age and people on the ramp acquiring star status. Whether you are a politician or businessman having to interact with fans in close encounters, where the smile matters, money matters will not come in your way. For giving a person the confidence to go through life, flash a smile and just look good. Practice of the techniques of tantropathy may be just as important as receiving a good education. It helps in elevating the mind, creating positive energy balance in the body, and raising the body's basal metabolic rate (B.M.R.).

::::::::

TANTROPATHY
GYAN-DHYAN MUDRA TECHNIQUE

Modern life is full of stresses and strains and it is natural for the people to want quick-fix method for relaxation and for that they need not use alcohol, smoking or chew tobacco. There are so many short-cut techniques in tantropathy among which Gyan-Dhyan mudra technique is simple but most effective. It helps the mind and body to relax maximum. In this technique, you have simply to unwind, be realigned, pampered, soothed and re-energised. Give some time to recover through technique and you will perform better for the whole day. This technique works on the pressure points of the body along the meridian channels of energy and for that you need only 3 to 5 minutes and all you require is a blanket to sit on the floor.

Procedure of Gyan-Dhyan mudra technique

Sit in Sukhasana (Comfortable posture) or stand in Tadasana in Welcome pose (Abhinanadanatmak mudra)

while folding hands from the elbow, giving pressure on all fingers and touching the Anaahad Chakra, but open your both hands up to wrist, stretching all the fingers to maximum extent. Foot soles of legs should also touch each other, but open the foot soles up to ankles and stretch all toes to the maximum for a few seconds and relax. Then bend your middle finger to touch the palm, then root of thumb and then the last phalange of the thumb. Stay for a few seconds in this pose and then relax. Repeat it thrice. If you know any mantra repeat for a few minutes and follow your daily routine. Om mantra can be used for this purpose.

::::::::

TANTROPATHY
AUTO SUGGESTION TECHNIQUE IN SELF HYPNOSIS

The life span can be extended by practising the techniques of tantropathy, especially Shubh Bhawana, regularly, making the life easier and longer. Techniques of tantropathy are stepping-stones to make your time stretch. If you are too lazy to change your bad habits and faulty life style, the good news for you is that there are a few tantropathic tricks. Here are some of the weired, wonderful and scientifically proven theories on things that add years to your life. 'Subha Bahwana and Prarthana (Prayer)' techniques are certainly life strengthening, *Durga Saptashati* is full of such prayers.

In Shuba Bhawana technique we fill our mind positively with positive ideas by auto suggestion, and condition the mind to think in that direction, inhibiting negative thought or to see the positive aspect in negative ones. The famous Russian psychologist Pavlova conducted a scientific experiment on a dog, to whom he gave food after ringing bell. After a few days he saw surprisingly that after hearing the sound of the bell, saliva from the mouth of the dog was flowing profusely if the food was delayed after ringing the bell. And he proposed the theory of 'conditioned learning'. It is an inherent nature of mind to be conditioned with any stimuli, whether environment, personal idea or emotions. If we are adjusted with any favourable or adverse environment, circumstances, persons or ideas, that is the capacity of conditioned learning. This capacity of learning was recognised by our rishis, munis and tantric, and the great Indian tantric culture is the outcome of that.

TANTROPATHY

It was known to Indian tantrics thousands of years ago that above the Agya Chakra there is the most sensitive part of the body in the middle of forehead, which has links not only with our physical mind but also with Sukhshm Sharir and is the source of extra-sensory perception. It was shown in tantra symbolically as the third eye of Lord Shiva and Shakti. Shakti and Shiva are the both ends of the same rope. When it is expressed through our body it makes us healthy (Shaktiman), and if it is expressed through our mind, it provides healthy, attractive, pleasing and acceptable personality. Such a personality was of our gurus, rhishis and munis.

Shubh Bhawana technique should be practiced along with 'Isht Pranam' technique, especially in the morning or if you have time in the evening also. It requires the practice of positive thinking for developing sense of appreciation and sense of tolerance and is the practice of spirituality. Hence model daily routine must be followed by the beginners. Practice should be done rhythmically and continually, and uniformity should be maintained from beginning to end. The meanings of verse or mantra should also be known clearly. The model Shubh Bhawana verse is as follows:

1. Niranjano ham, Jagadiswaro ham,
   Sushakti samarth yuto Hamisah.
   Niramayo ham, Ajramaro ham,
   Susundro ham dhanikah Kurberah.

(Being an integral part of supreme consciousness, I am same as beautiful, wealthy, healthy, enough powerful to do for the benefit of the society. I am the master of universe in subtle form).

2. Aham Param Brahm yuvakamarh.
   Prasanna Anand Mayo hamatma
   Vishadh vigyan ghanoti Nirmalah.
   Puranahchidanand Mayah Shevoham.

[Being a part of supreme consciousness, I am ever young as bachelor with thrilling pleasure, with smiling face, having quality of scientific and higher positive thinking as Purnasachidananda (Lord Shiva)].

3. Pathih Patinang Parmeshworoham.
   Bhupashya Bhupo Bhuwaneshwaroham
   Aham Ishwaranam Sarveshwaroham,
   Vandhan vimukto Muktesh waroham.

(Being a part of supreme consciousness, negative thinking, anxiety, stresses and strain which are detrimental to my health, fitness and happiness cannot overpower me because of the integral part of the Parmeshwara, Bhuwaneshwara, Ishwara and Sarveshwara).

Shubha Bhawana or prayer should be repeated before leaving the bed and after going to the bed. Sit in Virasana as well as Prayer mudra and you will see a magic effect on your body and mind within 30 days of practice.

National Institute of Health Research in America claims after long observation and experimentation that praying for long life could work miracles. A research report conducted by the institute reveals that church goers have a lower mortality rate. No doubt, comfort, hopes, success and support help in lowering mortality. But Daniel Weeks, a clinical psychologist at the Royal Edinburgh Hospital found in his observation and believes: "It is spirituality that counts". He further states that any form of faith, be it mysticism or even witchcraft, is life strengthening. Tantra says, "Prani Paten, Pariprashnen sewaya," meaning surrender completely before Isht, which may be person (guru) or the larger aims and objects (Pranipaten). Being an integral part of supreme consciousness, we are connected and related with the nature and society physically, mentally and spiritually, which we belong in particular and human society as a whole in general. Therefore we will be well equipped with all the ways and means of the development, search the solution of all the day-to-day problems (Pariprashnen) and to serve the society selflessly as its responsible member (Sewaya). True spirit of sewaya is that if you want to do good for yourself, do good to others. Practice Shubh Bhawana technique along with 'Isht Pranam' with any form of faith or belief which certainly life strengthening (longevity) and harbinger of prosperity. Tantra further declares that mudra and human feelings have innate relations. Any feeling whether good or bad will have and produce corresponding poses and postures. Similarly, if poses are practiced regularly, they would produce corresponding feelings immediately.

::::::::

MEDITATION TECHNIQUE

The process of obsevational meditation for medicinal purposes is as follows, especially for heart disease. You have to require only a photo of a person you respect, who may be mother, father or guru, and a blanket.

First stage: You have to stand comfortably with smiling face, bending hands from elbow and joining both palms touching chest in Abhinandanatmak mudra (Welcome pose) for 3 minutes only. Eyes to be kept half opened, seeing your own nose watching your respiration without interfering. The pressure of your body will be on your hips.

Figure-1

Second stage: You have to sit in Virasana (Hero pose) on a blanketed floor in front of the photo of your respectable personality. Bending from your knee, touch the ground and sit on your heel with buttock comfortably. Raise your both hands above the head and stretch and touch the ground with palms in the same posture as Welcome pose (Ardh Pranam) and watch your respiration without interference for 3 minutes.

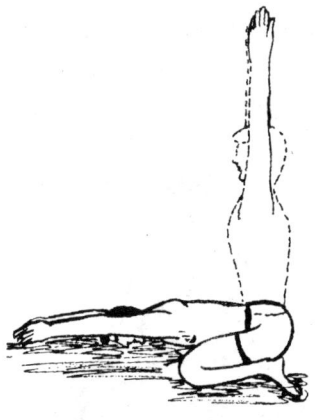

Figure-2

Third stage: Lie down on the floor covered with carpet or blanket, with abdomen touching eight organs of the

Figure-3

body in surrender pose (Sashtang Pranam). The eight organs are head cavity, thorax cavity, abdomen cavity, pelvic cavity, both hands and both legs. Watch your respiration without interfering for 3 minutes or more, simultaneously reciting mantra: Om Namah Shivaye, or Soham.

Fourth Stage: Sit comfortably in any meditative pose like Siddhasana, Sukhasana or Virasana, with half-open eyes and crossed fingers in the lap for 10 minutes and watch your breathing coming in and going out.

Figure-4

One way to do that is to focus gently on something, which has natural or positive connotation for you. The focus should not be on an idea that can be thought, but on something that is simply repeated over and over simple words (Beej Mantra) connecting with own breathing. Normal thought should not creep in occasionally, otherwise it will be a total failure. It will be okay to leave it behind and continue the practice. Regular practitioner will have stress-free feelings even for the whole day after 10 minutes of practice. Before leaving the bed and after going to bed is the best time for practising this meditation technique.

TANTROPATHY

MODEL LIFE STYLE FOR HEALTH AND FITNESS

Style of life represents the present life of human-being. If you remain ill or unhealthy, you have adopted a faulty life style under the influence of modern culture and customs in particular, and from the family members, class-mates, colleagues, relatives etc. by auto suggestion, prestige suggestion and mass suggestions in general. Mass suggestions are customs and cultural influences, whereas prestige suggestions are adoption of life style of prestigious people like religious leaders, political leaders, media persons and heroes in the eyes of adults as father, mother, elders or filmi heroes. People generally die from the effects of atherosclerosis, in which the arteries that carry blood to the heart are progressively clogged with fatty deposits until insufficient blood reaches heart and the person has a heart attack. The only widely accepted cure of this dangerous disease is to increase the flow of blood through the arteries either by balloon angioplasty or bypass surgery.

The age-old tantric culture of India is expressed through proverbs, idioms and simple sayings that show changes can benefit their heart and their overall health. These are "Per Garam, Pet Naram, Matha Thanda, Is par bhi Baidya Kahe Rogi, to Maro Usko Danda." (If your legs are warm, stomach is soft and head is cool, certainly you are a healthy person; and even then if any doctor announces you sick, he is a cheat and abuse him). Techniques of tantropathy are for keeping the head cool, making the abdomen soft and warming the legs. Modest style of life is daily routine for fitness and health, from leaving the bed to going to bed, with the practice of specific systematic techniques. To follow a system in daily life with reverence will not keep you healthy and fit. But systematise not only your life but business also. Try for a month only and then write to me about your happiness or torture. When a person is irritable, depressed or anxious it is blamed normally on stressful events or his natural temperament. But recent research unearthed another possible explanation for negative moods and behaviour — vitamin and mineral deficiency. Moods, emotions and behaviours are also influenced by mood-making chemicals or neuro-transmitters in the brain.

Four of these chemicals are produced directly from the food we eat, especially vegetarian food. Protein, vitamins 'B' and 'C', iron and magnesium are vital elements of these chemicals. Even moderate deficiencies of vitamin 'B' (thiamine, folic acid, 'B 6' and 'B 12') can bring about an unexpected grumpy feeling, depression and anxiety, and make the head hot. Apart from taking vegetarian food, exercises of eyes, vocal cord and muscles are essential for making the head cool, because mind is expressed through these. Hence these channels can be utilized for making the head cool or to influence the mood-making channels, the neuro-transmitters in the brain. As people in developing nations abandon their natural habits and pick up the life style of the developed countries, they also pick up new health risks.

According to the 1997 World Health Report published by the WHO, countries like India can expect the number of

TANTROPATHY

deaths by cancer, heart disease, stroke and diabetes to double in the next 25 years. These and all considered life-style diseases are associated with an inactive mechanised life, like obesity, and use of soft refined diets full of fat, red meat, tobacco and alcohol. It is feared that countries like India may end up adopting a life style that is worst of both the worlds, with the inadequate public hygiene common in developing nations and the soft life style of developed nations. Health experts warn that people in developing countries should be aware of the risks of Western habits. In such an alarming situation Indian people in particular and developing countries in general should adopt the age-old tantric life style (which we are producing here).

Our stomach should be soft for remaining fit and in good health, and for that Maha Mrityunjaya technique or practice of Isht Pranam are the best along with 'Baba Shaiya'. Chandrayan technique of tantropathy is the best weapon of self control. Psychologists have discovered through experiments that will power is strongest when you apply it to one task at a time and Chandrayan Vrat is the best way to develop will power. Attempts at showing self-control on too many fronts at the same time are likely to fall because they all draw on the same limited supply of strength.

The Nature follows a system. Without following system, we become unnatural. Systematic working and performing daily duties are the natural ways of doing the things. The way we think, work and see the things is our style of life. If we are not systematic in our day-to-day life, at home, in family and society, we cannot be systematic in our working or work place. We perform 90% of our duties habitually.

TANTROPATHY

Our style of life covers all these things. Actually in the words of famous Russian psychologist, Mr Pavlov, conditioned habits become life style in the long run. Style of life is such a defined boundary in which neither we allow others to peep, nor try to go out, forming healthy style of life. Tantra says from visiting lavatory to taking meal and going to sleep is worship for the people. This is the natural way of living. This is the system which everybody has to follow for remaining fit.

Model daily routine

1. (a) Wake up after 6 to 7 hours of sleeping in the morning, preferably before 7 a.m. Before leaving the bed take full-bloom "Angrai" (stretch the whole body slowly) in Sawarasana. Throw your legs and hands with the movement of your body left to right and right to left as well as stretch the hands and legs straight with open ankles and palms.

    (b) Then keep your heels on the floor and raise the forefront of your feet slowly as high as possible. Hold that position and count. Gradually lower the feet to the flat shorting position. Repeat it thrice. We should not forget that not only the face but also feet are the introduction of human being. Our feet are the most used and abused parts of our body. Each has 26 bones and bears the responsibility of your body weight. Your feet love to exercise and walking, and that is their favourite way to increase circulation and improve muscular tone. Try stretching the

Achilles tendons to relieve leg-muscle pain. Always give them new affection by massaging and walk, exerting pressure on hips.

2. Wash your mouth and eyes and drink two glasses of water, and in lavatory always use Indian system of commode for passing stool. Sit comfortably. Have deep breath from stomach after raising the head and then hold the breath and bend slightly forward, so that pressure should be on navel. Draw in the stomach as much as possible. Slowly contract the anus muslces just as horse does before and after passing the stool. Clench the jaws and grip handful. This process of anus contraction is called Bajikaran mudra. Repeat twice or thrice. In this process first gases will come out from the stomach and you would feel natural urge of passing the stool. This way you tone up the muscles of anus and pump sufficient blood supply to the area. Repeat this process till you have cleared satisfactory motion. It will take hardly 5 to 10 minutes.

3. Wash your hands properly, clean your teeth with brush, massage and clean your throat and inflate of the nose with your middle and index fingers by moving inward and outward and then upward and downward. In this way plenty of mucus will come out. If there is vomiting, no harm. Fill your mouth with a big gulp of water and then splash cold water in your eyes as many times as you can, while holding your breath. Spit the water out, take a fresh gulpful of water and repeat two

or three splashes. Gradually this practice will enable you to hold your breath longer. This routine is beneficial for your eyes as well as facial muscles.

(4) Then have a full naked bath, massaging from head to toes of your body at least five times. After pouring water and without rubbing the body, absorb water with towel. Stand in Tadasana in Abhinandanatmak mudra (Welcome pose), or concentrate on bulb, making sure that the bath room is well illuminated but softly lit. Quickly start your system. Feeling dreadful after an over-indulgent evening, an invigorating shower will get you back on track; shower until the skin is warm. Then switch the temperature to cool without rubbing the water with towel from the body, then put cold (10^0C) water for 15 seconds to 1 minute, then rub the body with towel and warm. This increases cardio-vasular output and stops potential hang-over. Perform Pitri Yagya (Pay reverence to forefather).

Rishis, yogis and tantrics have realised in Sadhana that there is Pret yoni and that worms and small insects are its crudest forms — which are called Bhutas. The greatest tantric of 20th century has called them microvita. There are three types of mocrovita, which are called Bhutas. There are three types of microvita, one which we can see with naked eyes, as various types of worms and insects which are spread through punch bhuta; the second that we can see with naked eyes but cannot feel when they attack, as H.I.V. viruses, T.B. viruses etc.; and third,

TANTROPATHY

the viruses which neither we can see with naked eyes nor we can feel when they attack but only spiritually involved person can realise them through idea and thought. We can identify them in two major groups: Negative ideas and thoughts attract unfriendly microvita, whereas positive ideas welcome friendly ones. Pitri yagya is designed with specific mudras, which are very much effective in inviting friendly microvita or maintaining the health and fitness, as follows.

Stand in Tadasana in Welcome mudra (with folded hands, wrist and fingers touching both thumbs in Anaahad chakra (bottom of the ribs cage). Utter slowly "Pitri Purushebhyo Namah" with open palms as if you are offering something to your dearest with reverence. Repeat "Rishi Dewebhyo Namah" with same mudra, "Brahmarpanam, Brahma Hawir Brahmna Graw Brahahutam". Reverse the open palms and utter "Brahmaiwa ten gantavyam, Brahm Karm Samadhina.' Repeat the Sanskrit verse thrice, concentrating on bulb

Figure

light and with mudras thrice. Then rub the body with towel, remove extra water from the body and after changing the clothes come into your bed-room.

5. Stand in Tadasana on a blanketed floor and start doing Isht Pranam. Ancient physician, Sushruta, talks in his *Sushruta Samhita* about certain pressure points and energy channels in our body, which when pressed automatically by postures and poses or by the experienced kith and kin or physician, eradicate diseases and tap energy. Our rishis and munis were practicing these and they remained hale and hearty. Isht Pranam is designed in such a way that they develop a strong immune system for regular practitioners and eradicate even prolonged diseases including AIDS. This technique succeeded by 90% in wide ranging diseases like respiratory disorders, spondylitis of all types of problems of indigestion, kidney and blood pressure, circulation of blood, diabetes, sciatica pain etc. Even psychological problems like depression, phobia, anxiety, hysteria and mental tension can be removed by practicing this technique. It requires only 10 to 15 minutes every day with unfailing regularity. Those who work in offices like administrators and clerks usually sit for hours together which gives pelvic a little tilt. This stresses the sciatic nerve and sets off pain in the lower back. Sitting for late hours with your legs crossed at the knees has the same effect. Back experts advise you to cross your legs at the ankles. Isht Pranam is best for

pelvis tilt, causing sciatic nerve and sets off pain in the lower back.

Even if you are agitated or stressed, the stream of nervous messages passing from the brain to the muscles speed up and you become physically and mentally tense without realising it. Many people who are under stress have permanently contracted muscles. This adds to the stress because the brain interprets the clenched muscles as a danger signal. It responds by sending out more nervous massages, which clench the muscles even together creating a vicious circle. Isht Pranam is designed to make relation easier but that should be practiced along with Shubh Bhawana. It also slows down the ageing process, by making you smart. Through the use of your brain you enjoy a longer life. Those who keep themselves mentally active as they get older by practicing Isht Pranam technique and follow the model routine remain smart forever. We should not forget that the brain needs regular exercise and if you do not use it, it becomes slack, which accelerates ageing process.

At the end, Tandava Nritya should be performed to jolt the whole system of the body and then relax. All this processes will take not more than 45 minutes and make you hale and healthy as well as give you pleasing and attractive personality. Then take cucumber, apple etc. with a glass of lemon tea as a breakfast and run to your office. Take meal at 1.30 positively and have a nap for 20 to 30 minutes. Again be ready at 2 to 2.30 for work. At evening you can enjoy light refreshment and by 10.30 finish your dinner, sit in Virasana for 2 to 5 minutes and then sleep in Baba Shaiya with Shubh Bhawana.

Make it a habit to take at least a glass of water before taking any solid thing or even tea or coffee. Aqua (water) has great power; drinking lots of water is great for your skin and for digestion and actually helps reduce cellulite. Drinking more than 8 glasses of water a day can reduce the risk of even cancer. You should not forget that regular practising the techniques of tantropathy (including Dharna and Dhyan) with change in life style and dietary habits can certainly help in preventing diseases and accelerate the healing process.

::::::::

GOOD HEALTH IS OUR NATURE

Tantra says: "Good health is our nature and it can come in a natural way". We become ill due to adoption of unnatural life style. Modern life has become demand of the day and modernisation has entered from kitchen to even bedroom. We usually suffer dehydration and lack of alkali, minerals and laxative in our body. Fruits and vegetables are natural and staple food of man. They contain substantial quantities of essential nutrients in a rational proportion. They are an excellent source of minerals, vitamins and enzymes. They are easily digested and exercise a cleansing effect on the blood and the digestive tract. Fresh fruits and vegetables are not only a good food but also a good medicine. They have hydrating, diuretic, alkalinising, mineralising and laxative effect and tonic action on body.

Nature has offered ready-made healing property in fresh fruits and vegetables along with delicious taste. In Indian tantric culture certain fruits and vegetables are offered to prominent deity and by this way, as prasad, it is binding for devotees to eat that. All berries and which are offered to Lord Shiva are rich in iron, phosphorus and sodium, and are highly beneficial for blood building and nerve strengthening. Amla, lemon and other citrus fruits and vegetables are remedy for inner ailments, indigestion and rheumatism. Apples, dates and mangoes have a direct action on the central nervous system. The total intake of liquid (water) should not be less than 6 to 8 glasses.

TANTROPATHY

Vegetables along with fruits are offered to Surya Deo especially cucumber, radish, sugarcane, spinach, coconut, lemon, apples, amla etc., which is the most pleasant way of hydrating. They have diuretic alkalinising, mineralising, laxative effects and tonic action. The water absorbed by sick person from juice has an added advantage of supplying sugar and minerals at the same time. Clinical observations have shown that potassium, magnesium and sodium contents of the fruits and vegetables act as a diuretic and diuresis; as a result frequency of urination is considerably increased. Fruits and vegetables have very low level of sodium, which makes valuable contribution to a salt-free diet.

The fibrous matter in fruits, cellulose, aids in the smooth passage of the food in the digestive tract and makes easy bowel action. Green fresh fruits and vegetables supply needed elements for the body's own healing activity and cell regeneration and thereby speed up the recovery. Several fruits like papaya and mango contain good amount of carotene, which gets converted to vitamins C and A in the body. Fresh and fully ripe fruits like grapes, apples, bananas and figs are best suited for all brain deficiencies. They contain a superior quality of easily assimilable sugar, which is transformed into physical energy that refreshes the brain.

Milk and adults

In India milk was considered the complete food for children, adolescents and even adults. But today a school of thought from U.S.A. is gaining wide acceptance that milk is actually bad for adults. "Milk is the root cause of many ailments in adults. Regular and prolonged intake of milk may result in diseases such as asthma, cold, a running nose, weak eyesight, cataract, indigestion, heart disease, arthritis and tumours". Further research reports that cow's milk contains casein, which adults find difficult to digest. Casein is broken down by an enzyme, called thymosin, which curiously is secreted only in a child's stomach. The fact that adults lack it indicates that milk is not meant for them. The only category who requires milk is the one who undertakes rigorous physical exercise, as he needs extra supplements of calcium and proteins.

But food and exercises have a tremendous influence over the body and mind, and no one can attain mastery over the mind without strict right balance of diet and exercise. We can observe the behaviour of mind after taking alcohol or a heavy sumptuous and indigestible rich meal, which generates a feeling of heaviness and arouses passion at the same time. We should not forget that we have to take our meal to maintain physical and mental efficiency and to keep our body in sound health, and that should be well balanced diet and not a senselessly rich one. Indian yogis believed that the food items have the quality to increase vitality, energy, vigour and health, filling you with joy and infusing with a warm cheer — like milk, barley, wheat, cereals, butter, tomato, honey, fruits, almonds, ginger, green vegetables and potato. Tea and coffee can be taken but in moderation. Food should be taken timely. Avoid overloading the stomach, eat in a quite and pleasant frame of mind, giving full attention to the food at regular intervals of at least 4 hours. Have plenty of water after meal. Salad must be taken along with meal, in which tomato, cucumber, carrot, lettuce and cauliflower must be added.

Anaemia is not associated with overwork for underfed people. Recent reseaches at M.S. University in Baroda show that Indian food is mostly cereal based and absorbtion of iron from such food is low. Due to this reason Indian women and school-going children are commonly anaemic. Even a fair diet can keep you short of iron. But fortunately a study at the same university found that one guava a day eaten at lunch and dinner raised haemoglobin level in 1 month from 10.7 gm/dl to 12.9 grams/dl, because it is a great source of vitamin C which helps you absorb most of the iron from your existing diet. You can get vitamin from lemon, oranges, any cilrus fruits and salad as long as it is uncooked and you should take it with the meal.

It is a fact that excess of every thing is bad and taking too much milk and butter for adults also causes obesity and abdominal ailments. Milk is medicine if we take less than 200 grams after night meal with honey. It works as a laxative and sedative.

Milk with honey applied on face regularly and washed with cold water can bring smoothness, softness and glow, which is the ultimate beauty asset. Nature has designed the skin to maintain itself, but pollutants in the atmosphere can be harmful to our skin.

However, taking milk is not harmful for all. No doubt it does not suit every body. People who are allergic to milk should avoid it, as also those watching their cholesterol level. It entirely depends on constitutional level of an individual. The patients of asthma and obesity should definitely avoid it. Ayurveda believes that milk helps in improving the human reproductive system. Some studies in the U.S. A suggest that a high intake of calcium (around 1200 mg) actually prevents high blood pressure and helps lower blood cholesterol levels, effectively slashing the bad cholesterol. Still others suggest that pre-menstrual syndrome in women, like pains, cramps and water retention are reduced with a high intake of calcium. By far the greatest benefit is in preventing osteoporosis, the gradual thinning and weakening of bones with age and more particularly with the onset of menopause in women. Calcium should be taken with vitamin 'D' for greater benefit in the form of milk and vegetable.

Aerobics have become the demand of the day but researches have found that those who did a combination of 15 minutes of aerobic and 15 minutes anaerobic exercises, at least three times a week, lost twice as much weight as those who confined themselves to 30 minutes of aerobic exercise. Techniques of tantropathy are the appropriate combination of both aerobic and anaerobic exercises and you can get quick results for overweight and obese people.

Health is considered a total sense of well-being in tantropathy, which in turn is physical, psychological, emotional and spiritual. Spirituality is the social sense of human being, which plays important role in keeping fit for a healthy life. What is the best diet, the best exercise and the best method of weight reduction are the questions which are most frequently asked by weight watchers and obese. Let us get to the first point. It is not important that what you eat and how much you eat, but how you hanker for eating, how much you avoid likely food (amritann) and how much liquid you are taking in a day, that determines how much you weigh. I have already explained amritann. Second point is the exercise. Researchers have found that those who did a combination of aerobic and anaerobic exercises three times a week lost twice as much weight as those who confined themselves to 30 minutes of areobic exercises.

The reason for this is that anaerobic exercises are muscle-building exercises, and muscle consumes more energy than fat pound for pound. Muscles burn 50 calories per hour, whereas fat burns just two. Anaerobic exercises are not only weight lifting, calisthenics and working out with weight machines and oversized rubber bands. Aerobic exercises are also important, although the number of calories burnt are fewer when compared to anaerobic exercises. The total benefit of aerobic exercises lies in the fact that fitter you become the more fat you burn even while resting. Tantra combines the spirit of both, combining postures, poses as well as mantra in tantra and it revives your metabolism for hours after your work out, because of its rhythmical continuity, unity and sequence. What is important is the techniques in combination. Practicing of the technique only for 15 to 20 minutes in morning and evening is more than sufficient for weight watchers and obese.

The next point is that how protruding stomach, bulging thighs and loss through diarrhoea can be reduced. According to researches spot exercising only improves muscle tone. The bulge will not go by doing only stomach exercise, but by daily routine combination with a diet low in fat as well as Shubh Bhawana technique.

    Iron deficiency anaemia is a neglected tragedy, which is not visible. Mild anaemia does not even send out warning signals, but it gets worse when you might feel fatigued, lethargic, vulnerable to infections and irritable. The disease can strike practically any one and any where. Our body has no way of excreting iron. However, iron is widely distributed in the tissues. The loss of cells from surface like the skin and the intestine leads to iron loss. Excessive physical activity or exercise can also make a person anaemic as the body uses up more iron. The body does not produce iron, rather it absorbs iron from the food one eats. So your diet is a crucial factor. The iron in the diet is of two types: haem Iron is present in red meat, fish and poultry is absorbed better and non-haem iron found in cereals and vegetables is absorbed poorly. To enconunter this we need plenty of vitamin 'C', for which citrus fruits or a glass of lemon juice after a meal is sufficient. Rice based diet is also a cause of iron deficiency because rice is poor source of iron. A mixed diet is better: along with salad and citrus fruits it is the best solution, and juice of raw spinach, coriander leaves, carrot and beet roots are the best ways to beat anaemia.

::::::::